STUDIES
IN
TIMOTHY

STUDIES IN TIMOTHY

N. W. Hutchings

Hearthstone Publishing Ltd.

P.O. Box 815 · Oklahoma City, Ok 73101

A Division Of
Southwest Radio Church Of The Air

On The Cover

The cover picture shows excavations of the main street at Ephesus. The occasion for the picture was during a tour to this area led by Rev. Hutchings.

The Apostle Paul ministered at Ephesus, and on one occasion thousands of occult books were brought from the library and burned. The front of the library building is still standing at the end of main street, as shown in the picture.

Paul put Timothy in charge of the church at Ephesus, and the apostle's epistles to him were to help him in his administrative duties and responsibilities.

All scripture references are from the King James Version unless otherwise stated.

Studies In Timothy
First Edition, 1990
Copyright © by **Hearthstone Publishing**
Oklahoma City, OK 73101

Printed in the United States of America

Published by:
Hearthstone Publishing
P.O. Box 1144
Oklahoma City, OK 73101

Library of Congress Catalog Card Number 90-82658
ISBN 0-9624517-2-X

Table of Contents

Prologue

There are three pastoral epistles: 1 Timothy, 2 Timothy, and Titus. This particular classification is given to these books due to the fact that they contain instructions for church government and an orderly execution of the Lord's work. Paul's first epistle to Timothy is not considered one of his prison epistles because there is no indication found within the epistle that Paul was in prison or under legal restraint by the Roman government. It is believed that Paul was released from prison in A.D. 63 and that he returned to Macedonia and Asia Minor, revisiting the churches of Philippi, Ephesus, Galatia, and possibly even returning to Jerusalem.

Paul was once again arrested in A.D. 67 and it was after his second imprisonment that he wrote his second letter to Timothy. The first epistle of Paul to Timothy is important to Christian faith and service because it contains important guidelines which, when adherred to, will keep the churches on the missionary road God intended: the preaching of the gospel for the salvation of souls. When churches depart from these guidelines, they then fall prey to satanic infiltration and are bent by the winds of false doctrine. The reason churches are in the apostate and materialistic condition they are today is because they have not remained faithful to the ordinances for church government contained in the pastoral epistles.

Part One

First Timothy

Chapter One

We begin our study by reading 1 Timothy 1:1-2:

"Paul, an apostle of Jesus Christ by the commandment of God our Saviour, and Lord Jesus Christ, which is our hope; Unto Timothy, my own son in the faith; Grace, mercy, and peace, from God our Father and Jesus Christ our Lord."

As in all of his epistles, with the exception of Philemon and Hebrews, Paul declares the uniqueness of the apostleship to which he was called. It has been contended by some that Paul had an inferiority complex concerning his apostleship because he was not chosen by the twelve apostles at Jerusalem. This is not true. Paul emphasized the manner in which he was called to be an apostle so that Christians would know that the gospel by which they are saved is by special revelation, and not connected with the law or Judaism. *"Paul, an apostle, (not of men, neither by man, but by Jesus Christ, and God the Father, who raised him from the dead;)"* (Gal. 1:1). Paul did not attempt to minister on the coattails of the twelve apostles or the Jerusalem assembly. He missed no opportunity to declare to the Gentile believers that his apostleship was not connected with the Jewish church and that his gospel was according to a new and divine revelation for a new dispensation: the dispensation of grace. We read in Galatians 1:11-17: *"But I certify you, brethren, that the gospel which was preached of me is not after man. For I neither received it of man, neither was I taught it, but by the revelation of Jesus Christ. For ye have heard of my conversation in time past in the Jews' religion, how that beyond measure I persecuted the church of God, and wasted it . . . But when it pleased God, who separated me from my mother's womb, and called me by his grace, To reveal his Son in me, that I might preach him among the heathen; immediately I conferred not with flesh and blood: Neither went I up to Jerusalem to them which were apostles before me; but I went into Arabia, and returned again unto Damascus."*

There were some who attempted to discredit Paul as a God-appointed witness to the Gentiles and the messenger of a new dispensation on the grounds that he had never even seen the Lord Jesus Christ; therefore, even the least of the Jerusalem assembly who had sat under the teaching of Jesus was better qualified than he. Paul dealt with these malicious charges in 1 Corinthians 9:1-4, *"Am I not an apostle? am I not free? have I not seen Jesus Christ our Lord? are not ye my work in the Lord? If I be not an apostle unto others, yet doubtless I am to you: for the seal of mine apostleship are ye in the Lord. Mine answer to them that do examine me is this. Have we not power to eat and to drink?"* Paul's declaration is that he had seen the Lord at the time of his experience on the road to Damascus. If he were not a duly appointed apostle to the Gentiles, how then could he have won to the Lord congregations which comprised the churches of Asia Minor and Macedonia? Paul states further in 1 Corinthians 9:5, *"Have we* [meaning himself] *not power* [authority] *to lead about a sister, a wife, as well as other apostles* [meaning the twelve apostles], *and as the brethren of the Lord* [James and Jude], *and Cephas* [Peter]?"

The entire Christian church was founded upon the missionary journeys of Paul and the gospel which he had received through revelation. We read in Ephesians 3:1-3, *"For this cause I Paul, the prisoner of Jesus Christ for you Gentiles, If ye have heard of the dispensation of the grace of God which is given me to you-ward: How that by revelation he made known unto me the mystery. . . . "* And so for our obedience in the faith and Christian service, for ordinances concerning church government, and the carrying on of the Lord's work during the dispensation of grace we go to the pastoral epistles of Paul.

Once Paul sets forth his credentials of apostleship, he identifies himself as the author of the epistle. He then addresses the letter to Timothy, as his name is given in the Hebrew, or Timotheus, as it is written in the Greek. We are introduced to Timothy in Acts 16:1, *"Then came he* [Paul] *to Derbe and Lystra: and, behold, a certain disciple was there, named Timotheus, the son of a certain woman, which was a Jewess, and believed; but his father was a Greek.* " In 2 Timothy 1:5, Paul informs us that Timothy's mother's name was Eunice and his grandmother's name was Lois. The name of Timothy's father is not given because it is evident that he was an unbeliever and probably numbered among the idol worshippers of Greece. Paul, being a gentleman, ignores the father rather than grieving his friend in the faith by saying anything unkind about him.

In 1 Timothy 1:2, we notice that Paul refers to Timothy as his own son in the faith. This is commonly interpreted to mean that Paul led Timothy to a saving faith in Jesus Christ. We read in Acts 16:1 that when Paul first met Timothy, he (Timothy) was already a disciple of Christ, but this is in no way a contradiction. The word *disciple* means "learner" and does not indicate a state of salvation. The disciples of Christ were the ones who followed after Him. Timothy was interested in the teachings of Christ, but it was Paul who informed the young man that Christ died for his sins and that he would be saved from death unto life if he would receive Jesus Christ as his personal Savior.

The revelation committed to Paul gave him the authority to instruct the twelve apostles, and even the brothers of Jesus, in a fuller understanding of the mystery concerning the dispensation of grace. The particulars of this dispensation were a mystery to the apostles because they were looking for the Kingdom age. We read in Galatians 2:1-2, *"Then fourteen years after I went up again to Jerusalem with Barnabas, and took Titus with me also. And I went up by revelation, and communicated unto them that gospel which I preach among the Gentiles, but privately to them which were of reputation. . . ."*

Peter acknowledged the authority of Paul in 2 Peter 3:14-16, *"Wherefore, beloved, seeing that ye look for such things, be diligent that ye may be found of him in peace, without spot, and blameless. And account that the longsuffering of our Lord is salvation; even as our beloved brother Paul also according to the wisdom given unto him hath written unto you; As also in all his epistles, speaking in them of these things; in which are some things hard to be understood. . . ."*

Peter acknowledged that Paul had received great wisdom from the Lord concerning the message of salvation by grace through faith in Jesus Christ, but Peter admitted that many facets of this Pauline revelation were difficult to understand. Although difficult to understand, the divine revelation committed to Paul and his authority to instruct the Gentiles in the way of salvation was never questioned by the twelve apostles. Even quick-tempered Peter meekly submitted to Paul's reprimand as we read in Galatians 2:11, *"But when Peter was come to Antioch, I withstood him to the face, because he was to be blamed."* If the apostles and the brothers of Jesus were instructed by Paul concerning the gospel of grace and the salvation of the Gentiles, certainly Christians and congregations should explicitly follow those instructions given in the pastoral epistles.

We continue by reading 1 Timothy 1:3-4:"

"As I besought thee to abide still at Ephesus, when I went into Macedonia, that thou mightest charge some that they teach no other doctrine, Neither give heed to fables and endless genealogies, which minister questions, rather than godly edifying which is in faith: so do."

After Paul met this young disciple of Christ at Lystra, and doubtless brought him to accept the Lord Jesus Christ as Savior, Paul took Timothy with him on his second missionary journey. We read of Timothy in Acts 16:3-5: *"Him would Paul have to go forth with him; and took and circumcised him because of the Jews which were in those quarters: for they knew all that his father was a Greek. And as they went through the cities, they delivered them the decrees for to keep, that were ordained of the apostles and elders which were at Jerusalem. And so were the churches established in the faith, and increased in number daily."*

One may wonder why Paul would circumcise Timothy when he later wrote in Galatians 5:2-4, *"Behold, I Paul say unto you, that if ye be circumcised, Christ shall profit you nothing. For I testify again to every man that is circumcised, that he is a debtor to do the whole law. Christ is become of no effect unto you, whosoever of you are justified by the law; ye are fallen from grace.*"

When Paul first began his mission of taking the gospel of grace to the Gentiles he ran into a great deal of trouble with disciples of the Jerusalem church. Paul was teaching and preaching that salvation was by grace through faith, and we read in Acts 15:1 that some Jewish disciples rebuked him, saying that unless he circumcised believers according to the law, they could not be saved. Paul subsequently went up to Jerusalem to discuss this matter with the apostles. At the famous Jerusalem council (Acts 15:1-32), they arrived at an agreement whereby the Gentiles would refrain from committing acts that were particularly abominable to the Jews. Although Paul was careful not to offend the Jewish community (this is why he took young Timothy to be circumcised), he continued to minister a gospel of grace rather than law, as James points out in Acts 21:21, *"And they are informed of thee, that thou teachest all the Jews which are among the Gentiles to forsake Moses, saying that they ought not to circumcise their children, neither to walk after the customs."*

Aside from Paul, Timothy was perhaps the most prominent leader in the first century Gentile Christian church. Paul first met Timothy at Lystra in the year A.D. 51, at which time Timothy must have been in his late teens or early twenties. Paul was so impressed that he took Timothy with him when he continued his journey. From Lystra, Paul and Timothy traveled to

Troas, Philippi, Thessalonica, and Berea preaching the gospel and founding churches wherever they went. Paul gradually began to entrust important work to Timothy and left him at Berea for Christian service, later sending for him to come to Athens. The church at Thessalonica was suffering severe trials. Paul could not return to the brethren of this church because he would have been killed on sight by the Jews and idol-makers, so he sent Timothy, as we read in 1 Thessalonians 3:1-2, *"Wherefore when we could no longer forbear, we thought it good to be left at Athens alone; And sent Timotheus, our brother, and minister of God, and our fellowlabourer in the gospel of Christ, to establish you, and to comfort you concerning your faith."*

By the time Timothy returned to Athens to rejoin Paul, the apostle had left for Corinth. Timothy later joined Paul in Macedonia and it was from here that they wrote the second epistle to the church at Corinth. We read in 2 Corinthians 1:1, *"Paul, an apostle of Jesus Christ by the will of God, and Timothy our brother, unto the church of God which is at Corinth. . . ."* From Macedonia, Timothy journeyed with Paul to Asia Minor on the apostle's way back to Jerusalem, but whether he went with Paul all the way to Jerusalem is not certain. It appears that he probably did, because from Paul's prison epistles it is apparent that Timothy was with him in Rome, probably in the same place of confinement. We read in Philippians 1:1, *"Paul and Timotheus, the servants of*

Jesus Christ, to all the saints in Christ Jesus which are at Philippi, with the bishops and deacons. " It appears that both Paul and Timothy were released from prison at about the same time in A.D. 63, as we read in Hebrews 13:23-24, *"Know ye that our brother Timothy is set at liberty; with whom, if he come shortly, I will see you. Salute all them that have the rule over you, and all the saints. They of Italy salute you. "*

It would seem that Paul and Timothy did not travel eastward together, or if they did so they became separated, otherwise there would have been no necessity for this first epistle to Timothy. We must remember that Timothy's work was primarily the training of pastors and congregational leaders. There were no seminaries to supply Paul with trained pastors. They had to be educated and confirmed in the faith within a matter of days or weeks at most. Yet in spite of this difficulty, the church grew and prospered. During the imprisonment of Timothy and Paul, a great need for pastors and church workers arose, and Timothy hastened to help alleviate these needs. From this we see the importance of the ministry of Timothy, for many of the churches during this period were pastored by men who were personally instructed in their doctrine and duties by him. It is no wonder that Paul considered him a most valuable fellow-servant in the Lord Jesus Christ.

It would appear from the Pauline epistles that Timothy was a shy and retiring fellow who shunned controversy and troublemakers. He was not as gifted in handling troublemakers as Titus was, and his dedication to the great responsibilities which were placed upon him, plus his nervous nature, evidently brought on a chronic stomach affliction, possibly an ulcer. We read in Paul's instructions to Timothy in 1 Timothy 5:23, *"Drink no longer water, but use a little wine for thy stomach's sake and thine often infirmities."* Next we read 1 Timothy 1:5-6:

> *"Now the end of the commandment is charity out of a pure heart, and of a good conscience, and of faith unfeigned: From which some having swerved have turned aside unto vain jangling."*

We conclude from Paul's opening remarks in this epistle that Timothy had returned to Ephesus after he was released from prison. Although there is no outright declaration to this effect, the inference is strong enough to support our conclusion. Paul recalls to Timothy's mind his sworn duties to teach no other doctrine from that which he had committed to him and to weed out those who go off on tangents and indulge in endless genealogies and fables. There are some in our midst today who continue to do this very thing.

The purpose for the genealogies in the Old Testament was to trace the blood line of descent from the first Adam to the second Adam, and the royal ancestry from Abraham to David to Christ. These genealogies ended with Matthew 1:16, *"And Jacob begat Joseph the husband of Mary, of whom was born Jesus, who is called Christ."* Christ was the last Adam and the Messiah of Israel — Lord of lords and King of kings. There was no need for the keeping of future genealogies, for they all ended in Christ. Jesus Christ was the last of the royal line who had a right to the throne of Israel, and He left no descendants.

Paul compares those who would dwell on things not relevant to the dispensation of grace to noise makers or those who produce "vain jangling." Vain jangling means not making any sense, or not constituting a pattern of reason. We refer to the modern rock and roll or the heavy metal music as vain jangling, and that is exactly what it is — there is no meter, rhyme, or reason to it. The same is true of those who preach and teach doctrines not relevant to our times — they are out of step, out of place, and what they say is not pertinent. Like those who indulge in vain janglings, their words make no sense. They are masters of confusion.

Let us again read verse five, *"Now the end of the commandment is charity out of a pure heart, and of a good conscience, and of faith unfeigned."* The word in the Greek text for commandment used here is not the same word used for a commandment of the law. The word used by Paul means charge or pastoral responsibility. What Paul meant here was that the purpose of Timothy's ministry, or the ministry of any pastor for that matter, was to bring out the love of

Christ in the members of the congregations so that they might influence the unsaved and lead them to become Christians. The Greek word for charity here is *agape*, which simply means love, the same word translated "loved" in John 3:16. This does not mean teaching the church membership to be good social workers. It means to share the love of God abroad — the love which caused God to give His only begotten Son so that anyone who believes in Him can be saved.

A second desired result of a pastor's ministry is to bring a good conscience to the church membership. A pastor who does not lead and exhort the membership to study, to attend church, to carry on personal evangelism, and to give to the Lord's word is not doing his job properly. A good conscience toward God is obtained only through prayer, Bible study, witnessing, and giving. When the general membership does not have this good conscience, or sense of well-being, you have a cold, spiritless, dissatisfied, quarreling membership.

The third desired result of the ministry of a pastor is bringing the membership to a position of "faith unfeigned." This means an open and declared faith in the divine authority of the Scriptures, and an open profession of the Lord Jesus Christ as Lord and Savior. This means an outgoing Christian spirit that literally overflows and influences those around you. An unfeigned faith is the opposite of a hypocritical or pretended faith.

Timothy was a good pastor and a diligent bishop.

It is possible that the church at Ephesus remained more faithful to the charge committed by Paul than all of the other churches in Asia Minor. We read in Revelation 2:1-3, *"Unto the angel of the church of Ephesus write; These things saith he that holdeth the seven stars in his right hand, who walketh in the midst of the seven golden candlesticks; I know thy works, and thy labour, and thy patience, and how thou canst not bear them which are evil: and thou hast tried them which say they are apostles, and are not, and hast found them liars: And hast borne, and hast patience, and for my name's sake hast laboured, and hast not fainted."*

While we believe the messages to the seven churches of Asia Minor have an end-time application, we also believe that they reflect the condition of these churches at the time John was given the revelation in A.D. 96. We do not know how long Timothy remained at Ephesus. The last epistle that Paul wrote was his second letter to Timothy which we believe was completed in A.D. 68 or 69. In any event, it was written only a few weeks and possibly only a few days before Paul's execution by command of the Roman Emperor Nero. Concerning Timothy, we read in 2 Timothy 4:9-12: *"Do thy diligence to come shortly unto me: For Demas hath forsaken me, having loved this present world, and is departed unto Thessalonica; Crescens to Galatia, Titus unto Dalmatia. Only Luke is with me. Take Mark, and bring him with thee: for he is profitable to me for the ministry. And Tychicus have I sent to Ephesus."*

Just before his execution, all of Paul's helpers had left him with the exception of Luke, so Paul sent Tychicus to Ephesus as a replacement for Timothy, and insructed Timothy to come to see him as quickly as possible, bringing Mark with him. We simply do not know if Timothy and Mark arrived in Rome in time to see Paul before he was killed. We do know that Mark went to Rome at the command of Paul and it would seem evident that Timothy came with him. It was from Rome that Mark wrote the Gospel According to Mark, which was written primarily for the Romans. I believe that according to the last verse of Mark's gospel that it was written after Paul's death. It would seem that Timothy was the bishop of the church at Ephesus from A.D. 64 until A.D. 68.

Without doubt, he was a good bishop and even thirty years later this church was still the most fundamental of all the churches in Asia. Even so, it had departed from one of the important precepts of the Christian faith that Timothy had nourished among them —love. We read in Revelation 2:4, *"Nevertheless I have somewhat against thee, because thou hast left thy first love."* Some may wonder what kind of a love their first love was. Was it a love for the Lord Jesus Christ, a love for mission, a love for Bible study, a love for lost souls? I think all we have to do to determine what kind of love they had lost is to consider the love that Paul nourished in Timothy. Reading again 1 Timothy 1:5, *"Now the end of the commandment* [pastoral charge] *is charity* [love] *out of a pure heart, and of a good conscience, and of faith unfeigned."*

The church at Ephesus had lost the ability to communicate the love of God as mentioned in Romans 5:5-6, *"And hope maketh not ashamed; because the love of God is shed abroad in our hearts by the Holy Ghost which is given unto us. For when we were yet without strength, in due time Christ died for the ungodly."* Like so many of our churches today, they had ceased to be an extension of God's love.

We should pray for all pastors who are faithful to their charge — the charge which Paul committed to Timothy. Many pulpits are today filled with apostates — wolves in sheep's clothing. But we do praise God for the Timothys of our day.

We ask our Christian friends to search their hearts. Are you sharing the love of God with others? Do you have a good conscience toward God? Are you satisfied with your own testimony and service? Do you manifest a "faith unfeigned"? If you possess a positive Christian attitude, why not call someone today who is in trouble and needs Jesus, and tell them that God loves them and explain to them how God sent His only begotten Son to deliver them from the penalty of sin. Never forget to pray for those who are in the forefront fighting the good fight of faith and share with them a portion of that which the Lord has blessed you. Above all, say a good word about Jesus today. Let everyone know that you are a Christian and that you praise God for so great a salvation in the Lord Jesus Christ. If you manifest an unfeigned faith, then others will want to possess what you have.

> *"Desiring to be teachers of the law; understanding neither what they say, nor whereof they affirm. But we know that the law is good, if a man use it lawfully; Knowing this, that the law is not made for a righteous man, but for the lawless and disobedient, for the ungodly and for sinners, for unholy and profane, for murderers of fathers and murderers of mothers, for manslayers, For whoremongers, for them that defile themselves with mankind, for menstealers, for liars, for perjured persons, and if there be any other thing that is contrary to sound doctrine; According to the glorious gospel of the blessed God, which was committed to my trust"* (1 Tim. 1:7-11).

Paul was apprehensive of law-keepers frustrating the gospel of grace which he preached among the Gentiles. The churches of Asia Minor were particularly susceptible to those from Israel who came preaching the law of Moses for righteousness. This was a continually delicate matter between Paul and the Jerusalem assembly. The church at Jerusalem remained Jewish and Kingdom age in their ministry.

When Paul returned to Jerusalem, James met him with these words in Acts 21:20, *"And when they heard it, they glorified the Lord, and said unto him, Thou seest, brother, how many thousands of Jews there are which believe; and they are all zealous of the law."* Members of the Jerusalem assembly often went into Asia Minor and when they would present themselves at a Gentile church they would be welcomed wholeheartedly and given a hearing. Invariably they would teach the law of Moses for righteousness. These are the ones of whom Paul spoke in Galatians 1:8, *"But though we, or an angel from heaven, preach any other gospel unto you than that which we have preached unto you, let him be accursed."*

Paul had good reasons for being fearful of those members of the Jewish church who tried to mix the gospel of the kingdom with the gospel of grace. We read in Galatians 3:1-6, *"O foolish Galatians, who hath bewitched you, that ye should not obey the truth, before whose eyes Jesus Christ hath been evidently set forth, crucified among you? This only would I learn of you, Received ye the Spirit by the works of the law, or by the hearing of faith? Are ye so foolish? having begun in the Spirit, are ye now made perfect by the flesh? Have ye suffered so many things in vain? if it be yet in vain. He therefore that ministereth to you the Spirit, and worketh miracles among you, doeth he it by the works of the law, or by the hearing of faith? Even as Abraham believed God, and it was accounted to him for righteousness."*

Why was Paul so disturbed? The church at Galatia had been subverted from the truth of the gospel of Christ by Jewish disciples and had reverted back to the keeping of the law for righteousness. We read in Galatians 2:21, *"I do not frustrate the grace of God: for if righteousness come by the law, then Christ is dead in vain."* Paul told the Galatians that if they intended to try and keep the law for righteousness they might as well forget about Jesus Christ. They had completely frustrated the gospel of grace. Paul said in Romans 11:6, *"And if by grace, then is it no more of works: otherwise grace is no more grace. But if it be of works, then is it no more grace: otherwise work is no more work."*

Some say it is all right to accept the gospel of grace by believing on the Lord Jesus Christ as Savior, but that this is only the first step to salvation. From there you must be baptized, join the church, and keep the commandments and the ordinances of the church. But Paul says salvation, by legal definition, must be *all* of grace or *all* of works. It cannot be a combination of the two. We refer again to Ephesians 2:8-10, *"For by grace are ye saved through faith; and that not of yourselves: it is the gift of God: Not of works, lest any man should boast. For we are his workmanship, created in Christ Jesus unto good works, which God hath before ordained that we should walk in them."* Once again we are presented scriptural proof that Christians are saved in order to work, they do not work to get saved. So Paul warns Timothy to be ever on guard against those who would mix the law with grace.

Paul continues to explain that he has nothing against the law, if the law is kept in its proper place. But the place of the law is not in condemning an innocent man. We read in Romans 5:1, 8-9, *"Therefore being justified by faith, we have peace with God through our Lord Jesus Christ . . . But God commandeth his love toward us, in that, while we were yet sinners, Christ died for us. Much more then, being now justified by his blood, we shall be saved from wrath through him."* To be justified means "to be found innocent or guiltless before the law." Christians are innocent before the law because Christ died and shed His blood for the guilt of those who would believe on His name. Paul said the law is for the lawless and not the innocent.

Suppose a police officer approached a man on the street, opened up the statute book, and said to the man, "I see here we have on the books a law against murder; therefore, I am going to charge you with murder." The man would then protest his innocence to the officer and the officer would reply, "Well, if you are innocent of murder then you can go to court and try to prove you never killed anyone." The officer would then continue to charge some with armed robbery, others with theft, prostitution, and so on. You would protest that this officer was using the law unlawfully. And this is exactly what Paul says here in 1 Timothy. When you attempt to charge Christians under the commandments of the law, you are using the law illegally because you are accusing someone who has already been justified before the law. Paul declared in 1 Corinthians 15:3, *"For I delivered unto you first of all that which I also received, how that Christ died for our sins according to the scriptures."* Christ has already been accused, tried, convicted, and executed for the sins of Christians; therefore, when a Christian is condemned by the law, he is placed in "double jeopardy". This would be an attempt to try him twice for the same crime.

Now we come to the same old question that has been asked millions of times. Can Christians willfully transgress the commandments of the law? Can they curse, drink, steal, lie, commit adultery and fornication, and get away with it? Of course not! When a church member seeks to satisfy the "lust of the flesh" and the "pride of life" by committing carnal deeds condemned by the law, we must seriously question whether or not that person is truly a born-again believer. We read in Romans 6:1-2, *"What shall we say then? Shall we continue in sin, that grace may abound? God forbid. How shall we, that are dead to sin, live any longer therein?"* We read also in Romans 6:17-18, *"But God be thanked, that ye were the servants of sin, but ye have obeyed from the heart that form of doctrine which was delivered you. Being then made free from sin, ye became the servants of righteousness."* Thus, Christians being made free from the penalty of sin are saved by grace to become the servants of righteousness rather than remain the slaves of sin. You might say, "Well, I don't see many Christians today who are the servants of righteousness." In replying, I would say that you see church members and professing believers, but not many Christians. Now, I certainly do not imply that Christians live above sin and never commit sin, but when you see professing believers living in a sinful condition with no desire for the fruits of righteousness, then we should question whether or not they have ever truly received the Lord Jesus Christ as Lord and Savior.

So Paul admonished Timothy, the bishop at Ephesus, to be on guard against all who would contradict the glorious gospel of God's sovereign grace that He had. The gospel of grace was committed to Paul's trust and Paul guarded it jealously against all who would attempt to distort or frustrate it with other doctrines. Grace is mentioned ten times more in the Pauline epistles and Acts, in conjunction with Paul's ministry, than it is mentioned in the other fifty-three books of the Bible.

> *"And I thank Christ Jesus our Lord, who hath enabled me, for that he counted me faithful, putting me into the ministry; Who was before a blasphemer, and a persecutor, and injurious: but I obtained mercy, because I did it ignorantly in unbelief. And the grace of our Lord was exceeding abundant with*

faith and love which is in Christ Jesus" (1
Tim. 1:12-14).

In all Israel there was no stronger opponent of
the Lord Jesus Christ and His disciples than Saul of
Tarsus. Paul says that he was a "Hebrew among the
Hebrews," meaning there was no more fanatical
advocate of historic Judaism than he. In 1 Timothy
1:13 Paul states that he was a blasphemer against
Christ — he cursed Christ and the disciples and called
them every vile name he could think of. We also read
that he, as a young member of the Sanhedrin and an
astute law graduate of the Jerusalem law school, was
appointed the prosecutor of the church at Jerusalem.
We read in Acts 8:1-3, *"And Saul was consenting unto
his death* [meaning Stephen]. *And at that time there
was a great persecution against the church which was
at Jerusalem; and they were all scattered abroad
throughout the regions of Judaea and Samaria,
except the apostles. And devout men carried Stephen
to his burial, and made great lamentation over him.
As for Saul, he made havock of the church, entering
into every house, and haling men and women
committed them to prison."*
Paul was injurious to the disciples — he killed
the saints. We read in Acts 9:1, *"And Saul, yet
breathing out threatenings and slaughter against the
disciples of the Lord, went unto the high priest."* Paul
was at war with the Lord Jesus Christ and to him the
disciples were the army of this imposter who dared to

criticize the religion and laws of his beloved Israel and prophesy of its coming destruction. We don't know exactly why Paul held such a vicious hatred against Jesus Christ and His church. Some believe that Paul was the rich young ruler whom Jesus commanded to sell all he had, give it to the poor, and become a disciple. Paul was rich, he was young, and he was a ruler — a member of the Sanhedrin. If Paul was this rich young ruler, then Christ saw that his riches, his power, and his pride stood between him and God, and this could have been the reason Paul became such a malicious enemy of Christ and the church. But, Paul says he persecuted the church out of ignorance — he did not know what he was doing. There is a difference between attacking the faith and the faithful out of ignorance and doing it with full knowledge. An apostate is one who works from inside the church to destroy the precepts and doctrines of the church. Jude calls them twice dead — condemned to eternal outer darkness. I have never known of an apostate who has repented of his deeds and accepted Christ as Savior.

We read in 1 Timothy 1:15-16:

"This is a faithful saying, and worthy of all acceptation, that Christ Jesus came into the world to save sinners; of whom I am chief. Howbeit for this cause I obtained mercy, that in me first Jesus Christ might shew forth all longsuffering, for a pattern to them which should hereafter believe on him to life

everlasting."

We read in Romans 8:7 that the carnal man is at war with God. Like Paul, if you are not a Christian, you too are at enmity with God and His Christ. But Jesus did not come into the world to save the righteous. He came to save sinners. Paul said that if His love and grace is wide enough and deep enough to save him, then He will save anyone who believes on His name. If you are not a Christian, will you receive the Lord Jesus Christ as your Savior today and, like Paul, find peace with God and inherit life everlasting?

Paul was arrested once again in A.D. 67. Whether he was arrested in Macedonia, Asia Minor, or Israel and returned to Rome, or whether being disheartened, he returned to his church at Rome of his own free will is not certain. In any event, we know from Paul's second epistle to Timothy that he was again in prison in Rome during the fall of A.D. 67 or the winter of A.D. 68. We read in 2 Timothy 4:9-13, *"Do thy diligence to come shortly unto me: For Demas hath forsaken me, having loved this present world, and is departed unto Thessalonica; Crescens to Galatia, Titus unto Dalmatia. Only Luke is with me. Take Mark, and bring him with thee: for he is profitable to me for the ministry . . . The cloke that I left at Troas with Carpus, when thou comest, bring with thee. . . ."*

From this we see that it was getting cold in Rome when Paul wrote his last epistle for he needed his coat. This also indicates that Paul was definitely in Asia

Minor because he was at Troas, which later became Constantinople, or Istanbul as it is known today.

Let us again read 1 Timothy 1:15-16, *"This is a faithful saying, and worthy of all acceptation, that Christ Jesus came into the world to save sinners; of whom I am chief. Howbeit for this cause I obtained mercy, that in me first Jesus Christ might shew forth all longsuffering, for a pattern to them which should hereafter believe on him to life everlasting."*

The word for faithful in the Greek text is *pistos,* which means trusted, or the absolute truth, something that cannot be disputed or questioned. *Pistos* in the Greek is similar to *petros,* meaning a rock, or a rock foundation. Jesus said that upon the rock foundation of Peter's declaration that Jesus was the Christ, the Son of God, would He build His church. In other words, Paul was telling Timothy that the foundation and mission of the Christian church stood upon the divine truth that Jesus came into the world to save sinners. Jesus did not come into the world and die on the cross to bring racial, social, or economic equality. He came into the world to save sinners from an everlasting Hell unto everlasting life. The reason the church is falling apart today is because its leaders have departed from this foundation to build upon the shifting sands of social cause.

Paul used the expression, "a faithful saying," in only three verses of scripture in all his epistles. All three are found in the pastoral epistles of Timothy and Titus, and in all three instances he refers to the foundation of the church. The second place it is found is in 2 Timothy 2:10-11, *"Therefore I endure all things for the elect's sakes, that they may also obtain the salvation which is in Christ Jesus with eternal glory. It is a faithful saying: For if we be dead with him, we shall also live with him."* This was a restatement of Paul's declaration in Galatians 2:20-21, *"I am crucified with Christ: nevertheless I live; yet not I, but Christ liveth in me: and the life which I now live in the flesh I live by the faith of the Son of God, who loved me, and gave himself for me. I do not frustrate the grace of God: for if righteousness come by the law, then Christ is dead in vain."*

The essence of this truth is that Christ died for our sins, and when we accept Him as our Savior, then we too, meaning the old self, are crucified with Christ on the cross and God counts us as having died for our sin. Then the life which was in Christ, eternal life, is given to us and the saints stand righteous, holy, and sinless before the throne of Heaven. To believe otherwise is to frustrate the gospel of grace. It is a sad thing that the vast majority of churches today are controlled by bishops, pastors, and deacons who have frustrated the gospel of grace. But Paul says that a good pastor will not do this — he will stand on the foundation of rock, the Lord Jesus Christ.

The third place that Paul uses the expression "a faithful saying" is in Titus 3:5-8, *"Not by works of righteousness which we have done, but according to his mercy he saved us, by the washing of regeneration, and renewing of the Holy Ghost; Which he shed on us abundantly through Jesus Christ our Saviour; That being justified by his grace, we should be made heirs according to the hope of eternal life. This is a faithful saying, and these things I will that thou affirm constantly, that they which have believed in God might be careful to maintain good works. . . ."*

A true minister of the gospel and pastor of a church will stand on this foundation, and not only stand, but constantly affirm and preach that this is what he believes. The mission of the church is to save sinners, declaring that they are saved not by works, but according to the mercy of God in sending Jesus Christ to die in their place. It is not according to water baptism or any work which they might do, but according to faith in Jesus Christ whereby they are created a "new creature" in Christ by the regenerating power of the Holy Spirit. Paul continues and qualifies his statement about works to affirm that those who believe (the saved), should be careful and diligent to maintain a high degree of good works, again presenting the truth that men are saved to work for God's purpose, they do not work for salvation.

Again reading 1 Timothy 1:15, *"This is a faithful saying, and worthy of all acceptation, that Christ Jesus came into the world to save sinners; of whom I am chief."* Now, who is a sinner? We read in Romans 3:22-23, *". . . the righteousness of God which is by faith of Jesus Christ unto all and upon all them that believe: for there is no difference: For all have sinned, and come short of the glory of God."* Therefore, Jesus Christ came into the world to save you — regardless of who you are or where you are. Christ died for your sins and if you believe on Him and receive Him as your Savior, you will be saved.

Let us again read 1 Timothy 1:16, *"Howbeit for this cause* [meaning to declare this message to the Gentiles] *I obtained mercy, that in me first Jesus Christ might shew forth all longsuffering, for a pattern to them which should hereafter believe on him to life everlasting."* Some interpret this to mean that because Paul was such a mean person and had persecuted the church, that Jesus Christ appeared to him personally and saved him to show men that if God was willing to grant mercy to Paul, He will grant it to anyone. Certainly, we agree one hundred percent with this interpretation as far as it goes; however, we believe it does not go far enough. Only Paul was given an absolute ministry to the Gentiles. Only Paul claimed to have received the gospel of salvation for the Gentiles. Only Paul received a message for the Gentiles that was divorced from the covenants that God made with Israel concerning the kingdom on earth. The message that Jesus preached was for the salvation of the lost sheep of the house of Israel. Jesus said to the Gentile woman with a sick child, *". . . I am not sent but unto the lost sheep of the house of Israel"* (Matt. 15:24). We read also in Romans 15:8-9, *". . . Jesus Christ was a minister of the circumcision for the truth of God, to confirm the promises made unto the fathers: And that the Gentiles might glorify God for his mercy; as it is written, For this cause I will confess to thee among the Gentiles, and sing unto thy name."* Paul declares himself as the one whom God called to confess Christ to the Gentiles. We read in Romans 15:16, *"That I should be the minister of Jesus Christ to the Gentiles, ministering the gospel of God, that the offering up of the Gentiles might be acceptable, being sanctified by the Holy Ghost."* We also read in Ephesians 3:1-5, *"For this cause I Paul, the prisoner of Jesus Christ for you Gentiles, If ye have heard of the dispensation of the grace of God which is given me to you-ward: How that by revelation he made known unto me the mystery . . . Which in other ages was not made known unto the sons of men. . . ."*

Thus, for church doctrine and obedience in the faith, pastors need to follow the truths set forth by Paul. It was for this cause that Paul went to the Gentiles establishing churches wherever he went, and it was for this mission that Jesus Christ personally appeared to the apostle. When Paul later declared in his second epistle to Timothy that all the churches in Asia had turned against him, it was actually more than a personal rejection; it was also a rejection of the gospel of God's sovereign grace. They had followed the example in the church at Galatia and frustrated the mission of the church by reverting back to a stress on works for salvation. It is the rejection of the Pauline revelation within the church today that has caused the divisions in doctrine and the frustration.

We continue now by reading 1 Timothy 1:18-20:

"This charge I commit unto thee, son Timothy, according to the prophecies which went before on thee, that thou by them mightest war a good warfare; Holding faith, and a good conscience; which some having put away concerning faith have made shipwreck: Of whom is Hymenaeus and Alexander; whom I have delivered unto Satan, that they may learn not to blaspheme."

The more ministers depart from that simple gospel of grace — that Christ came into the world to save sinners and that salvation is by faith in what He accomplished on the cross — the more apt they are to go into apostasy and blaspheme His name by spurning the blood atonement. The blasphemy, which began even in Paul's day, permeates most of the larger denominations. Paul wrote in 2 Timothy 2:16-18, *". . . for they will increase unto more ungodliness. And their word will eat as doth a canker: of whom is Hymenaeus and Philetus; Who concerning the truth have erred, saying that the resurrection is past already; and overthrow the faith of some."*

The rapture, or the resurrection of the church, was part of the mystery that was committed to Paul. While resurrections are dealt with in general in the Old Testament and the gospels, only Paul tells of the order of the church in the raising of the dead.

Blasphemers such as Hymenaeus who contradicted the gospel preached by Paul were turned over to Satan by Paul because they had made a shipwreck of their ministries.

Let us again read 1 Timothy 1:18-20, *"This charge I commit unto thee, son Timothy, according to the prophecies which went before on thee, that thou by them mightest war a good warfare; Holding faith, and a good conscience; which some having put away concerning faith have made shipwreck: Of whom is Hymenaeus and Alexander; whom I have delivered unto Satan, that they may learn not to blaspheme."*

Take note that Paul reminds Timothy of "the prophecies which went before on thee." The meaning of this statement is explained in 1 Timothy 4:11-14, *"These things command and teach. Let no man despise thy youth; but be thou an example of the believers, in word, in conversation, in charity* [love], *in spirit, in faith, in purity. Till I come, give attendance to reading, to exhortation, to doctrine. Neglect not the gift that is in thee, which was given thee by prophecy, with the laying on of the hands of the presbytery."* Timothy had a particular gift to teach the Word and to maintain the membership in the faith. This gift was revealed to the presbytery, a group of elders in the church, and they chose Timothy as a bishop by the laying on of hands. They foresaw that Timothy had the ability and the dedication to be a good pastor. Paul, in giving fatherly advice to young Timothy, reminded him that he had a grave responsibility to God and the membership of the church, and should he fail in his duties, he would be failing those who selected him for this office. Paul said, "this charge I commit unto thee." The charge was to be faithful to that gospel which Paul had delivered unto him. Every pastor, every minister, every bishop and deacon has the same responsibility — to declare that Jesus Christ died for sinners and that salvation is by faith according to God's grace.

Next we come to another rather perplexing statement made by Paul in verse twenty. He said he delivered to Satan two pastors who had disputed and taught contrary to the gospel. Now, we have to determine just what is involved in turning a blasphemer, especially those in high authority, over to Satan. This action not only concerns blasphemers, but those who bring discredit upon other Christians through shameful personal conduct. Paul stated in 2 Corinthians 13:2, *"I told you before, and foretell you, as if I were present, the second time; and being absent now I write to them which heretofore have sinned, and to all other, that, if I come again, I will not spare."*

More light is shed on this subject by Paul in 1 Corinthians 5:1-2, 5, *"It is reported commonly that there is fornication among you . . . And ye are puffed up, and have not rather mourned, that he that hath done this deed might be taken away from among you . . . To deliver such an one unto Satan for the destruction of the flesh, that the spirit may be saved in the day of the Lord Jesus."* It is evident that when

Paul wrote to Timothy that the two apostates were delivered to Satan for blasphemy, he meant they were officially disassociated from the church, or as some call it, excommunicated. As Paul wrote in 2 Timothy 2:16-18, if they were left in the church this would indicate either a tolerance or an acceptance of their apostasy, or any other gross sin, and they would not only continue in their apostate teachings, but they would "increase unto more ungodliness."

There is today a general attitude of tolerance in our remaining fundamental churches toward those who blaspheme the gospel. Over and over we hear the statement that the church is big enough to absorb those of many beliefs, but this is not what the Bible teaches. Paul said that such men should be removed from membership and this is not only for the good of the church, but for the good of the sinners and apostates. If the church continues to give sanction to their iniquity, then they will never come to the knowledge of the truth and be saved. We do not believe that Paul was referring to saved people within the church as in his first epistles to the Corinthians when he dealt with carnal and worldly Christians in love and patience. He referred to these willful blasphemers and sinners as those "among you." Jude referred to the apostates and false teachers as those who "crept in unawares." By admonishing Timothy to deliver them to Satan he meant to get them out of the church and back into the world. We read in 1 Corinthians 4:4 that Satan is "the god of this world."

The thought Paul held was that if they were cast back into the world, the sin which they were inclined to commit would run its course, and perhaps they would realize their error and truly believe on Christ as their Lord and Savior.

Chapter Two

"I exhort therefore, that, first of all, supplications, prayers, intercessions, and giving of thanks, be made for all men; For kings, and for all that are in authority; that we may lead a quiet and peaceable life in all godliness and honesty. For this is good and acceptable in the sight of God our Saviour; Who will have all men to be saved, and to come unto the knowledge of the truth. For there is one God, and one mediator between God and men, the man Christ Jesus; Who gave himself a ransom for all, to be testified in due time" (1 Tim. 2:1-6).

In 1 Timothy 1:17, Paul referred to the Christians' King — the eternal and invisible God who rules over the universe from His throne in Heaven. Such statements were not welcomed by officials of the Roman government because they looked upon Caesar not only as king over the entire Roman Empire, but as a god. It may have been statements like this that ultimately resulted in Paul's execution. Certainly it was the failure of the Christians to bow down and worship Caesar that was responsible for their great persecution by the state. This was of great concern to Paul, and so it has been ever since that time. The political situation in a nation does affect the spiritual condition of the church. All we have to do to affirm this statement is to point to Russia and China. Therefore, in the administration of church business, Paul turns from the subject of maintaining good pastors who are grounded in the faith, to the relationship between church and state.

Paul sets forth human government as a divine institution because it was ordained by God. Before the flood there was no government. Everyone did that which was right in his own eyes. Violence and crime filled the earth. Therefore, for the sake of order and so that those who would might seek God in peace and truth, God instituted human government. The basic law of human government is capital punishment. Capital punishment maintains the sacred right of man to his own life. It is not a case of the state depriving the murderer of his life, but rather a case of the state protecting the lives of the innocent. The law of capital punishment in no way gives the state the right to take the life of a man for political or religious reasons. And in the area of human government, state officials are the ministers of God, just as pastors are ministers of God in the spiritual realm. A state official may or may not be a Christian, but even if he is not a Christian, this in no way affects his position as a minister of God in government. We read in Romans 13:1-4, *"Let every soul be subject unto the higher powers. For there is no power but of God: the powers that be are ordained of God. Whosoever therefore resisteth the power, resisteth the ordinance of God: and they that resist shall receive to themselves damnation. For rulers are not a terror to good works, but to the evil. Wilt thou then not be afraid of the power? do that which is good, and thou shalt have praise of the same: For he is the minister of God to thee for good. But if thou do that which is evil, be afraid; for he beareth not the sword in vain: for he is the minister of God, a revenger to execute wrath upon him that doeth evil."*

Just as there are apostates in the church, there are apostates in human government. These are the ones who overstep their bounds of authority seeking to subjugate the masses, and use their authority to enlarge their own political ideology or the geographical boundaries of their nations. The highest calling of human government, as stated by Paul in 1 Timothy 2:4, is to maintain a free society whereby the truth of God can be disseminated and all those who will hear and believe can come to the knowledge of the truth and be saved. But there are always kings and governments who seek to overstep the bounds which God has laid down, especially in many of the nations today. This is why we read this prophecy in Psalm 2 concerning the second coming of Christ: *"Why do the heathen rage, and the people imagine a vain thing? The kings of the earth set themselves, and the rulers take counsel together against the Lord, and against his anointed, saying, Let us break their bands asunder, and cast away their cords from us. He that sitteth in the heavens shall laugh: the Lord shall have them in derision. Then shall he speak unto them in his wrath, and vex them in his sore displeasure. Yet have I set my king upon my holy hill of Zion"* (Ps. 2:1-6).

But Paul would have us be at peace with the government of the nations in which we reside, and he would also have us pray for the leaders in government so that we Christians might be free to carry on the business of the church by preaching the gospel for the salvation of souls. This in no way infers that the church has either a right or an obligation to get involved in politics, nor does it mean that Christians should bow down to the demands of government when that government intervenes illegally in the affairs of the church. Paul harbored no illusions concerning apostates in government for there are many references in his epistles to the peril offered by the Roman government. The emperor Nero was a type of Antichrist and he directed a merciless slaughter of the Christians in Rome and in the provinces. Nero ascended the throne of Rome in A.D. 54, and in that same year Paul wrote, in his second epistle to the Thessalonians, "the mystery of iniquity doth already work." This "mystery of iniquity" will come to the full in the revived Roman Empire, and its ruler will be the Antichrist. Nevertheless, Paul instructs those Christians who lived in nations that permit religious liberty to thank God for their government and to pray for its leaders. Certainly, Christians in the United States have always been most fortunate in this respect, and we should always pray for those in positions of authority.

The closing two verses, 1 Timothy 2:5-6, of Paul's dissertation on the relationship of church and state are given so that Christians will not be led into Caesar worship. He declares that government cannot intercede for men before God, because only the Mediator between God and man can do this. Because Jesus gave Himself on the cross as a ransom for all, He is this Mediator. In those days, prisoners could be ransomed by their families for a price, and here Paul likens all men as being prisoners of sin under the sentence of death, but they can be ransomed for this penalty if they receive Christ as their Redeemer. All men and women stand condemned on death row, and there is only one man who can pay their ransom — the man Christ Jesus.

In 1 Timothy 2:7-8, we read:

> *"Whereunto I am ordained a preacher, and an apostle, (I speak the truth in Christ, and lie not;) a teacher of the Gentiles in faith and verity. I will therefore that men pray every where, lifting up holy hands, without wrath and doubting."*

For the cause of declaring to the Gentiles that they had a Mediator between God and man, Paul was called to be their apostle. An apostle is one who acts for another in Christ's absense. Thus, Paul was commissioned and called by Jesus Christ to teach the Gentiles about his great truth — that Christ the Lord had offered Himself as a ransom in their stead. And again we note that Paul defends his apostleship as he does in all cases where he refers to his high calling. As we have mentioned before, the right of Paul to be an apostle to the Gentiles was constantly challenged by the jealous disciples of Jewish background, because Paul was not appointed by the assembly at Jerusalem. Paul's appointment came by the direct appearance of the Lord Jesus Christ on the road from Jerusalem to Damascus, and he preached the gospel which he received by revelation from the Lord. So even lest his closest friend Timothy would be misled by this propaganda during his absence, Paul felt it necessary to again affirm his right and calling to set forth church doctrine for the Gentile churches. Paul's reference to the lifting up of holy hands in prayer refers to particular delegations of the most respected and dedicated leaders of the church. Today, we would refer to them as a prayer band within the church. It was often the manner of prayer in the East to hold up hands toward Heaven, pleading divine intervention. This was especially the manner of prayer in times of great persecution. In pictures smuggled out of communist countries, you can see Christians in a state of travail, holding up their hands toward Heaven in prayer. This reference by Paul was doubtless a veiled reference to the growing persecution of the church by the Roman government in his day, and it refers back a couple of verses to the conduct of the church under state authority. Even in times of persecution by cruel and godless leaders of nations, Paul instructs the Christians to pray to God for help and not resort to wrath and doubting — that is, do not resort to the sword and even though it may appear that God has forsaken them at times, to remember that the Lord is always on the throne and that all wrongs will be righted in the day of the Lord Jesus Christ.

The next subject which Paul discusses is the role of women in the church. Paul deals with the duties of the male membership in 1 Timothy 3; but being a gentleman, he presents the female church members to us first. We read 1 Timothy 2:9-15:

> *"In like manner also, that women adorn themselves in modest apparel, with shame-facedness and sobriety; not with broided hair, or gold, or pearls, or costly array; But (which becometh women professing godli-ness) with good works. Let the woman learn in silence with all subjection. But I suffer not a woman to teach, nor to usurp authority over the man, but to be in silence. For Adam was first formed, then Eve. And Adam was not deceived, but the woman being deceived was in the transgression. Notwithstanding she shall be saved in childbearing, if they continue in faith and charity and holiness*

with sobriety."

This portion of Paul's instruction to the church is most interesting and appropriate for discussion because of the current so-called "women's liberation movement." Even prior to establishment of the movement, this was a highly controversial portion of Scripture because of the rising prominence of women in the social, religious, and political realms. Fifty years ago, a minister could stand in the pulpit and apply this ordinance relating to the position of the female in the church and family and no one would be offended; but today, most ministers have to compromise and say, "Well, we know it says this, but it really means something else." The problem with expounding on this particular portion of Paul's epistle to Timothy is that the apostle considered the God-ordained position of the woman in relation to the man: her family and her church from the creation of the female, looking forward to the resurrection in which there is neither male nor female. Christians today, however, want to appraise Paul's remarks from the present time, or in light of the position of women in the modern world. This is where the difficulty arises. Keep in mind that Paul was writing to women of the church at Ephesus and these instructions are to be applied generally to all Christian women.

We read again in verses nine and ten, *"In like manner also, that women adorn themselves in modest apparel, with shamefacedness and sobriety; not with broided hair, or gold, or pearls, or costly array; But (which becometh women professing godliness) with good works.* "The words "in like manner," mean that within the order of the church, particularly the assemblies, clothing and all attachments thereto, including hairstyles and jewelry are to be worn in a modest manner. Peter expressed himself on the subject in 1 Peter 3:1-6: *"Likewise, ye wives, be in subjection to your own husbands; that, if any obey not the word, they also may without the word be won by the conversation of the wives; While they behold your chaste conversation coupled with fear. Whose adorning let it not be that outward adorning of plaiting the hair, and of wearing of gold, or of putting on of apparel; But let it be the hidden man of the heart, in that which is not corruptible, even the ornament of a meek and quiet spirit, which is in the sight of God of great price. For after this manner in the old time the holy women also, who trusted in God, adorned themselves, being in subjection unto their own husbands: Even as Sara obeyed Abraham, calling him lord: whose daughters ye are, as long as ye do well, and are not afraid with any amazement."*

So we see that the "apostle to the circumcision," and the "apostle to the Gentiles" agreed in that godly women of the assembly should dress modestly. Paul did not instruct Christians to deliberately incur the displeasure of others by insulting their customs and traditions. In Romans 13 he said to render custom where custom is due. In some nations the plaiting of the hair is a national or racial custom, and in other nations the most faithful wives wear pearls. In the South Seas the women wear their hair frizzed out like a porcupine. In Africa the women may wear a simple sheath, while in India their dress may sweep the ground. So these instructions in dress must be understood in the light of Paul's other declarations on the subject. The key words are "modest," "shame-facedness," and "sobriety." Paul admonishes Christian women to be modest in dress in contrast to the dress of the world. The woman is to dress with "shame-facedness," that is, with relatively humble apparel — wearing nothing that could bring shame upon her church or her husband. And the final adjective used by Paul to describe the proper attitude in dress of a Christian woman is "sobriety," which simply means, in the Greek text, "common sense." In other words, there are limitations in dress which plain common sense regulates. Other limits in dress are given in the Old Testament. We read in Deuteronomy 22:5, *"The woman shall not wear that which pertaineth unto a man, neither shall a man put on a woman's garment: for all that do so are abomination unto the Lord thy God."*

The last reference made by Paul pertaining to dress is that women of the church should avoided "broided" hair, and the wearing of ornaments of gold, pearls, and (this is important) costly array. In other words, a Christian woman, regardless of her financial circumstances, should not go around looking like a walking jewelry display. This is contrary to the Christian spirit which all believers should demonstrate before the world.

There was much contention among the members of the church at Corinth concerning the manner of dress and the length that men and women should wear their hair. Paul brought a conclusion to the matter in 1 Corinthians 11:14-16, *"Doth not even nature itself teach you, that, if a man have long hair, it is a shame unto him? But if a woman have long hair, it is a glory to her: for her hair is given her for a covering. But if any man seem to be contentious, we have no such custom, neither the churches of God."* A man should keep his hair short in comparison to the woman's hair, which is to be relatively long. However, today this has been reversed. Men's hair is often longer than that of women, and we are told that this is a shame and an abomination to the Lord. But in any event, Paul declared that we are not to be overly contentious — that Christian conscience, modesty, and common sense should dictate our manner of dress, depending, of course, upon the customs and traditions of the nations.

We read again 1 Timothy 2:11-15, *"Let the woman learn in silence with all subjection. But I suffer not a woman to teach, nor to usurp authority over the man, but to be in silence. For Adam was first formed, then Eve. And Adam was not deceived, but the woman being deceived was in the transgression. Notwithstanding she shall be saved in childbearing, if they continue in faith and charity and holiness with sobriety."*

Satan approached the woman rather than the man because he knew it would be easier to deceive Eve than Adam. We believe that the Scriptures are plain in that women are not to be pastors of churches or interpret doctrine. Certainly, this does not mean that women cannot have an important role in the church. We note in Acts 18:26 that along with Aquila, Priscilla expounded the Word of God "more perfectly," and God has used many godly women to teach others. But, it is evident from the Greek text that Paul meant only that women were not to teach doctrine according to their own understanding, but rather to teach only the truth of the Word. The prominence of women, that is women exercising authority over the man in both the secular and religious world is one of the signs that we are living in the end of the age. Some denominations have even installed women as pastors and priests. We believe that this constitutes a direct violation of the instructions Paul set forth within his epistles to Timothy.

We believe that Paul gives clarity to his statement concerning women keeping silent in the churches in 1 Corinthians 14:33-35, *"For God is not the author of confusion, but of peace, as in all churches of the saints. Let your women keep silence in the churches: for it is not permitted unto them to speak; but they are commanded to be under obedience, as also saith the law. And if they will learn any thing, let them ask their husbands at home: for it is a shame for women to speak in the church."*

It is apparent from Paul's epistle that the church services were often disrupted so much by wives talking over the voice of the pastor that it became utter confusion and chaos, so Paul admonished the ladies to wait until after the services had been dismissed to discuss the sermon or teaching with their husbands. This was done for the sake of order in the church. Paul reminds Timothy that it is the duty of the pastor to keep order in the assembly so that everyone can hear the Word expounded, and this would be especially beneficial to any unsaved person in attendance. We realize that it can become extremely uncomfortable to keep silent for long periods of time, but nevertheless Paul admonished Christians to offer their bodies as a sacrifice to the Lord, meaning all of the body, the tongue as well.

Now we continue with 1 Timothy 2:12, as Paul discusses the role of the woman in the ministry of the church:, *". . . I suffer not a woman to teach, nor to usurp authority over the man, but to be in silence."* I think that with such scriptures as these it is well for us to consider the language of the Greek text, and I quote Dr. Kenneth Wuest, who was a teacher of the Greek text at Moody Bible Institute for many years:

"The kind of teacher Paul has in mind is spoken of in Acts 13:1, 1 Corinthians 12:28-29, and Ephesians 4:11, God-called, and

God-equipped teachers, recognized by the church as those having authority in the church in matters of doctrine and interpretation. This prohibition of a woman to be a teacher, does not include the teaching of classes of women, girls, or children in a Sunday school, for instance, but does prohibit the woman from being a pastor, or a doctrine teacher in a school. The expression, 'usurp authority,' Vincent says, is not a correct translation of the Greek word. It is rather, 'to exercise dominion over.' In the sphere of doctrinal disputes or questions of interpretation, where authoritative pronouncements are to be made, the woman is to keep silence."

There are many illustrations in the New Testament where women did teach and were used mightily of God; however, there is no example in the New Testament where a woman pastored a church. When Satan made his move to bring the human race under the curse of sin, he did not go to Adam because Paul indicates here that Satan would have been unable to deceive the man. Satan went to Eve and argued doctrine with her as we read in Genesis 3:1, ". . . *Yea, hath God said, Ye shall not eat of every tree of the garden?"*

Man was created to be a keeper of the garden, and God gave man the woman to be his helpmate.

Woman was created for the position of helpmate in the political and social realms, as well as the ecclesiastical. One of the foremost signs that we are living in the end of the age is this usurpation of man's authority by the woman. The prophet Isaiah foretold that in the last days children would rule over the parents and women would become leaders of nations. We read in Isaish 3:4-5, 9-12, *"And I will give children to be their princes, and babes shall rule over them. And the people shall be oppressed, every one by another, and every one by his neighbour: the child shall behave himself proudly against the ancient, and the base against the honourable . . . The shew of their countenance doth witness against them; and they declare their sin as Sodom, they hide it not. Woe unto their soul! for they have rewarded evil unto themselves . . . As for my people, children are their oppressors, and women rule over them. O my people, they which lead thee cause thee to err, and destroy the way of thy paths."*

My, what a picture of our day! Children ruling over their parents and rising up against governmental authority. Isaiah said even their countenance would testify against them, and we only need look around us today to see fulfillment of this prophecy. Isaiah also said the sin of Sodom would be declared right out in the open — the homosexual would no longer be considered an evil-doer. Well, what do we see today? Homosexuals are being married in the church, living together, and now they have announced plans to take over an entire county in one of the western states.

The last sign that Isaiah mentioned was the rising prominence of women. He said they would become rulers of nations, and even of God's people, Israel. During the past twenty years, women have held the highest positions of authority in England, India, and yes, Israel to mention only a few. The women's liberation movement is breaking out in nation after nation, and Christianity is being blamed for keeping the women in slavery, but let us not forget that it was Christ who delivered woman from the eternal bondage of sin for He is the truly great Liberator of men and women alike.

In the December 1968 edition of *The Gospel Truth*, we inserted an article concerning what the coming of Christ meant to motherhood, and I think it would be well for me to repeat it here.

"It was a cruel world into which Christ was born. Grim Herod waiting to destroy the newborn King, is a true picture of the attitude of the early world toward childhood and motherhood. The difference Christ has made in the world by His coming could not be better expressed than in a fragment of a letter written on June 17, 1 B.C., by Hilarion to his wife, Alis, concerning his own child about to be born. The letter reads:

" 'Hilarion to Alis, Many greetings . . . Be not distressed if at the general coming in I

> *remain at Alexandria. I pray thee and beseech thee take care of the little child, and as soon as we receive wages, I will send them to thee. . . . If it be a male baby, let it live. If it be a female, expose it.' "*

The awful Greek word *ekbale*, meaning cast out, or expose, is sufficient to measure the difference between the world with and without Christ. A few years ago, a group of distinguished historians amused themselves by writing a book called, *If, Or History Rewritten*. Some of the "ifs" discussed were: "If Lee had not lost the Battle of Gettysburg"; "If Booth had missed Lincoln"; "If Napoleon had escaped to America." However, the greatest "if" imaginable is, "If Christ had not come."

Such an "if" is almost too staggering for our minds. It is like imagining the world without a sunrise, or the heavens without a sky. As far as the woman is concerned, the coming of Christ freed her to love and cherish her children and not have them killed upon birth. The coming of Christ delivered a woman from being a mere piece of property — sold at public auction to the highest bidder or dealt for privately with her father. The coming of Christ meant that woman became an equal in marriage with the male in a helpmate position. Christ gave woman the right to motherhood — to keep her children, but now woman has claimed the right to rid herself of children through abortion. The world is reverting back to the cruelty mentioned in the letter of Hilarion to Alis.

Again, reading the last two verses of 1 Timothy 2, *"And Adam was not deceived, but the woman being deceived was in the transgression. Notwithstanding she shall be saved in childbearing, if they continue in faith and charity and holiness with sobriety."*

Now certainly, Paul did not mean that the bearing of children had anything to do with salvation of the soul. If this were true, no man could be saved. The reference here to the saving of the woman in childbearing dates back to the first transgression. When Adam and Eve sinned, God had no legal obligation to spare their lives. However, God purposed that Satan should not destroy His ultimate will for the human race. God created man to have dominion over the earth and to keep the garden, and for this purpose man was spared, even though his task was multiplied greatly because of his part in the transgression. We read in Genesis 3:17-19, *". . . cursed is the ground for thy sake; in sorrow shalt thou eat of it all the days of thy life; Thorns also and thistles shall it bring forth to thee . . . In the sweat of thy face shalt thou eat bread, till thou return unto the ground. . . ."* Eve was created to be a helpmate to man and to bear children with great joy and replenish the earth. God spared Eve so that woman might fulfill her destiny, and we know from history that she has, like Adam, paid dearly for her part in the original sin. We read in Genesis 3:16, *"Unto the woman he said, I will greatly multiply thy sorrow and thy conception; in sorrow thou shalt bring forth children; and thy desire shall be to thy husband, and he shall rule over thee."* It was woman who led man into transgression and from the woman, in childbearing, would come the one who would save both male and female from the penalty of sin. What the Savior prophesied in Genesis 3:15 was fulfilled in Luke 1:46-50, *"And Mary said, My soul doth magnify the Lord, And my spirit hath rejoiced in God my Saviour. For he hath regarded the low estate of his handmaiden: for, behold, from henceforth all generations shall call me blessed. For he that is mighty hath done to me great things; and holy is his name. And his mercy is on them that fear him from generation to generation."* Thus, woman was not only saved for childbearing, she, like the man, was saved by the life she brought into the world in the fulness of time, the Lord Jesus Christ who came into the world to save sinners.

Chapter Three

"This is a true saying, If a man desire the office of a bishop, he desireth a good work. A bishop then must be blameless, the husband of one wife, vigilant, sober, of good behaviour, given to hospitality, apt to teach; Not given to wine, no striker, not greedy of filthy lucre; but patient, not a brawler, not covetous; One that ruleth well his own house, having his children in subjection with all gravity; (For if a man know not how to rule his own house, how shall he take care of the church of God?) Not a novice, lest being lifted up with pride he fall into the condemnation of the devil. Moreover he must have a good report of them which are without; lest he fall into reproach and the snare of the devil" (1 Tim. 3:1-7).

In the third chapter Paul instructs bishop Timothy concerning the proper qualifications of church leaders — bishops and deacons. The office of bishop, as referred to by Paul, means one who is the overseer of the church. At Ephesus, on his way back to Jerusalem, Paul declared to the church leaders in Acts 20:28-30,

"Take heed therefore unto yourselves, and to all the flock, over the which the Holy Ghost hath made you overseers, to feed the church of God, which he hath purchased with his own blood. For I know this, that after my departing shall grievious wolves enter in among you, not sparing the flock. Also of your own selves shall men arise, speaking perverse things, to draw away disciples after them."

Paul's use of the word "disciple" here refers to learners. Every false cult thrives on those who know a little about the Bible, but not enough to "rightly divide" the Word. Like wolves who feed on the lame and the stragglers, they devour those who are weak in the faith with false doctrines. Thus, one of the principal duties of bishops is to keep out the wolves and to expel those among the membership who resort to blasphemy. However, when the wolves themselves are in positions of leadership, the only alternative presented is for the sheep to run for their lives. For the most part, churches have not heeded Paul's warnings concerning careful selection of church leaders. Paul said it is not enough for a man to merely *desire* the office of bishop; he must have certain basic qualifications, both doctrinal and personal.

Concerning personal qualifications, the bishops (and we must include pastors in this category) should be blameless in the following things.

First and foremost, he should be the husband of one wife. Now, those who have carefully studied the meaning of the Greek text in accordance with the customs of Paul's day differ on what exactly is meant by "the husband of one wife." Some contend that Paul meant a bishop should have been married only once, even if his wife were deceased. Others believe that, inasmuch as bigamy and polygamy were common in those days, Paul meant that the bishop should be married to only one woman at any one time. If his wife were deceased, his marrying again would not exempt him from the office. DUe to the fact that there is such a difference of opinion on this point, I will not attempt to draw a conclusion, except to point out that second marriages in Romans 7:2-3 are sanctioned in the case of separation by death, and even recommended to young widows in 1 Timothy 5:14.

A bishop should be vigilant; he should always be on guard against false prophets and false teachers, of good personal habits, and always extending a welcome to the church membership, whatever the needs may be. He must also have an aptitude for teaching the Word of God.

In verse three we come to a perplexing statement, "not given to wine." Paul wrote to Timothy, who was a bishop, to take a little wine "for his stomach's sake." As I have pointed out before, a good rule to follow in determining whether wine in the Scriptures means grape juice or an alcoholic beverage is the context within which it is used. If it is evident the wine referred to would make someone drunk, then it is fermented wine. If not, then count it as grape juice. So I believe Paul meant for Timothy to drink unfermented wine, while here in 1 Timothy 2:3 it is evident that he meant a bishop should not be a fermented wine drinker. Another qualification that a bishop should have is that he should not be violent or an advocate of violence. This would, of course, rule out all of the church leaders who are preaching revolution.

Another qualification is that the bishop should discipline his children and keep his own home under godly authority according to the Scriptures. The modernists today not only teach permissiveness, they encourage the children to rebel against parental authority. Paul states that the bishop should not be greedy of filthy lucre, and what is probably meant here is that he should not hold office simply for the salary that is connected with the job. It should be noted that young men are refraining from entering the ministry because of the low wage scales, and many others are leaving the ministry for higher paying jobs. Paul also warns against the appointment of a novice to such a high office. "Novice" is used in the Scriptures in reference to a newly planted palm tree, a young sprout, and like the newly planted palm tree, they are green on top with underdeveloped roots. Young sprouts swarm out of the hot-house liberal seminaries of this age with a head full of knowledge, but with no basic grounding in the fundamentals of the faith. And, as Paul declared, when they appear before their pulpit, they fall into the condemnation of the devil. We read in Ezekiel 28:17 that pride caused the fall of Lucifer, and the same applies to many of the seminary graduates of our day. They are swelled up in their own self-importance — they are going to save the world from social ills and racial prejudices, and *whomp*, down they go right along with the devil and all those who place their own schemes and ideas above the holy truth of God.

Last, but not least, a bishop must live as a testimony (have a good reputation) among the unchurched, that is the non-believers with whom he associates during the week. We are aware that the Scriptures say that if you love Jesus and keep His commandments, the world will hate you, but the world can hate you and yet respect you, or say of you as Pilate said of Jesus, "I find no fault in this man." Paul warns against becoming trapped in the devil's snare by seeking to be popular with the world by joining in with the unsaved in their ungodly habits and sins. Then, instead of being popular, they are held in contempt, because men will point an accusing finger at them and say, "Why should I wish to become a Christian; your actions prove that you are no better than we are."

Being a candidate for a high church office requires more than just being a Christian on Sunday. It requires Christian dedication seven days a week. If we were to limit pastorates to the qualifications enumerated by Paul, three-fourths of the pulpits in the churches of this nation would be empty this coming Sunday. We hear so much about modernism and apostasy in the churches today with the memberships blaming the seminaries and the denominational leadership, but ninety percent of the cause can be found right here in the third chapter of 1 Timothy. The church membership has been asleep and failed to be diligent in the appointment of pastors and church officials. If you do not have a voice in the selection of the man who is to pastor your church, then we suggest you find a church where you will have a voice.

In the first seven verses of the third chapter of 1 Timothy, Paul outlined to Timothy the personal and doctrinal qualifications that an overseer of the church should possess. The classification of bishops as referred to by Paul includes any type of church official above the office of deacon. Paul was the highest authority of the Gentile church in that day, and Paul confessed his own failings and shortcomings in all his epistles. There are, however, certain basic standards which must be observed in the selection of those who are to shepherd the flock. To find the exact reason the communists, liberals, apostates, and anarchists are taking over the church, we go to the third chapter of Timothy. The members became swelled up in materialistic pride, and wanted huge churches, million-dollar budgets, and a Beau Brummel of a pastor who would tell them what nice people they were. Paul wrote in 2 Timothy 4:2-4, *"Preach the word; be instant in season, out of season; reprove, rebuke, exhort with all longsuffering and doctrine. For the time will come when they will not endure sound doctrine; but after their own lusts shall they heap to themselves teachers, having itching ears; And they shall turn away their ears from the truth, and shall be turned unto fables."*

If a shepherd leaves his sheep without a dog to watch over them, or he fails to pen them up at night, the wolves will come and devour as many as possible and kill the others. You can't blame the wolves because this is according to their wild nature. Likewise, the ravening wolves of Satan who are taking over the sheepfolds of the flocks today can't be blamed because they are merely agents of the devil and doing the devil's bidding. The fault lies with the memberships of the modernistic churches. They have failed to be diligent, in accordance with Paul's warning to maintain the minimal moral and spiritual guidelines in the selection of pastors and church officials.

Let us read the roster of Paul's minimal requirements for deacons in 1 Timothy 3:8-13:

"Likewise must the deacons be grave, not double-tongued, not given to much wine, not greedy of fulthy lucre; Holding the mystery of the faith in a pure conscience. And let these also first be proved; then let them use the office of a deacon, being found blameless. Even so must their wives be grave, not slanderers, sober, faithful in all things. Let the deacons be the husbands of one wife, ruling their children and their own houses well. For they that have used the office of a deacon well purchase to themselves

a good degree, and great boldness in the faith which is in Christ Jesus."

The qualifications for a deacon are just about the same as for a bishop. It is somewhat difficult to determine the exact position in the churches that the deacons occupied in Paul's day. Some explain the difference between a deacon and a bishop by saying that the bishop had to attend to the spiritual welfare of the church, while the deacon was delegated the temporal responsibilities of the church — such as maintaining the place for worship, the raising of funds, the care of the needy members, praying for the sick, visitation, and like duties. We note there is no reference made to teaching aptitude as a prerequisite for a deacon. However, like the bishop, the deacon should be the husband of one wife, ruling over his family, and keeping his children in subjection with godly authority, not allowing his wife to gossip, and he must be blameless before the civil law. In other words, a deacon should be a decent, hard-working, and respected member of the community — not a hen-pecked type of milquetoast individual who is brow-beaten by a gossipy ill-tempered wife and unruly children. Such men cannot respect themselves, much less command the respect of others.

In verse nine Paul declares that a deacon is responsible for *"Holding the mystery of the faith in a pure conscience."* Of this verse, Vincent says,

"The mystery of faith is that truth which was

kept hidden from the world until revealed at the appointed time, and which is a secret to ordinary eyes, but is made known by divine revelation."

Who received this mystery concerning the church of the dispensation of God's sovereign grace? Paul, of course. We read again in Ephesians 3:2-3, 5, *"If ye have heard of the dispensation of the grace of God which is given me to you-ward: How that by revelation he made known unto me the mystery . . . Which in other ages was not made known unto the sons of men. . . ."* Paul meant that all church leaders should be able to *rightly divide* the Word and place the heritage of the church in its proper perspective within the eternal economy of God. The mystery of the church which was revealed to Paul is presented in his epistles for church doctrine and our obedience in the faith. It entails the truth that Jesus Christ came into the world to save sinners, and that salvation is according to God's mercy and grace through faith, and not of works. The mystery concerns the destiny of the church, meaning that Christians are bound for heavenly places — to inherit the heavens. And according to Paul, church officials, of whatever degree, should be able to declare the Pauline revelation for church doctrine without doubt or wavering.

Another word we notice included in the qualifications for deacons that is not mentioned in the qualifications for bishop is "double-tongued." And certainly, we surmise that Paul meant this to apply to all church officials. The word in the Greek text applies to the saying of one thing and yet meaning another, or disguising the true meaning of what you are saying with high sounding words and veiled references. In many churches today the congregations have no idea what the pastor is preaching. They use double-talk to hide their apostasy and revolutionary thinking. Paul declared that unless a church leader will say what he means in clear and simple language so that everyone can understand, you had better get rid of him. He is hiding behind something.

Another place where we find a slight variance in the qualifications between a bishop and a deacon is in verse eight where Paul declared that a deacon should not be given to much wine. Most fundamental scholars who have written commentaries on 1 Timothy simply ignore this reference because they do not want to go on record admitting that the Scriptures would give even a qualified endorsement to the use of fermented wine. We must, however, face the Word squarely and not attempt to bypass those portions that may not agree with our own personal beliefs. It is evident, within the context here that Paul meant fermented wine with an alcohol content. Bishops are not to be given to wine, which could indicate a total abstinence from all alcoholic beverages; but deacons were not to be barred from office if they drank a little wine. Now, this is plainly what the Scripture says here, and I do not intend to belabor this point. Certainly,

Paul did not advise deacons to drink wine, but he did not condemn them if they consumed a small quantity. We must remember that in Paul's time, wine was used for ceremonial purposes and the traditions of these nations included the drinking of wine with the evening meal. Paul did not live in a day when billboards lined the roads showing partially naked women holding out a glass of one hundred-proof whiskey or some other alcoholic beverage. There are scores of scriptures in the Bible warning of the dangers of alcohol, and those who truly want to be used of God in a mighty way will shun it. We read of John the Baptist in Luke 1:15, *"For he shall be great in the sight of the Lord, and shall drink neither wine nor strong drink; and he shall be filled with the Holy Ghost, even from his mother's womb."*

A striking difference between Paul's roster of qualifications for a bishop, and his qualifications for a deacon occurs in verse eleven. We read, *"Even so must their wives be grave, not slanderers, sober, faithful in all things."* The word here for wives in the Greek text means "woman," not wife, and without doubt refers to deaconesses. Although a woman is not to occupy the office of pastor and interpret doctrine in the church, there is nothing said against a woman becoming a deaconess, and in fact, there were many women serving on the board of deacons in the early churches. We read in Romans 16:1, *"I commend unto you Phebe our sister, which is a servant of the church which is at Cenchrea."* And later on in verse three of the same chapter, Paul says, *"Greet Priscilla and Aquila my helpers in Christ Jesus."* It is evident that Priscilla and Phebe both had an important part in the ministry of their church, and they served as deaconesses. Thus, Paul's reference of the silence of women in the church and their not teaching in the church must be qualified to mean silence in the general assembly, and while they may teach children and other women, they are not to interpret doctrine.

"These things write I unto thee, hoping to come unto thee shortly: But if I tarry long, that thou mayest know how thou oughtest to behave thyself in the house of God, which is the church of the living God, the pillar and ground of the truth" (1 Tim. 3:14-15).

As we have noted before, this epistle was written in A.D. 64 a few months after Paul and Timothy had been released from prison in Rome. Paul had sent Timothy to be the bishop over the church at Ephesus while he visited many of the churches which he had established in Macedonia and Asia Minor. Timothy was still young and probably not overly experienced in this position, so Paul wrote to his son in the faith as a father would and said, "I hope to come and see you before long, but in the meantime, you behave yourself like a bishop should in the church and faithfully obey these instructions I have given you for the proper administration of the business of the church." The reference here to the house of God means literally the membership of the church. It is doubtful if any of the churches at that time had regular church buildings. They met for services in the homes of the bishops and deacons. The church building itself is not a house of God; only the Temple can be called the Lord's house because it will be His house when He returns the second time. This reference to the house of God means the membership of the church, a body of "called out" worshippers of the Lord. This is the correct definition of a church. There are all kinds of churches. The children of Israel in the wilderness were called a church because they were called out of Egypt to become God's chosen people. The church to which Paul wrote is that body of believers who have believed on the Lord Jesus Christ during the dispensation of grace, who are called out to be a select body of God destined for a heavenly heritage.

> *"And without controversy great is the mystery of godliness: God was manifest in the flesh, justified in the Spirit, seen of angels, preached unto the Gentiles, believed on in the world, received up into glory."* (1 Tim. 3:16).

Paul says that without controversy, great is the mystery of godliness, referring to the incarnation of Jesus Christ, the Son of God, in human flesh. So great a mystery is the incarnation that it remains a mystery to the world today, and even to the majority of those who profess Him. It was a mystery in the day that Christ was tried in a Roman court and hung on the cross. We read in 1 Corinthians 2:7-8, *"But we speak the wisdom of God in a mystery, even the hidden wisdom, which God ordained before the world unto our glory: Which none of the princes of this world knew: for had they known it, they would not have crucified the Lord of glory."* The fact that God could be born into the world of a virgin to die for the sins of men is a mystery which the Jews stumbled over, the world turns away from, and the apostates scoff at. Nevertheless, we who have believed on His name have been born again unto eternal life knowing Jesus Christ was everything the Scriptures declared Him to be — the very Son of God who died for our sins on the cross. We read in 1 Corinthians 1:18, *"For the preaching of the cross is to them that perish foolishness; but unto us which are saved it is the power of God."* We know He arose from the grave and ascended back to the Father to intercede for those who accept His mercy and grace. We know because today He saves sinners. He delivers drug addicts from their demonic obsession, and we see those things which He said would come upon the earth before His return happening in our day. He said He would come back and save the world from those who would destroy it. Thus, we see with Paul, great is the mystery of Jesus Christ, but praise God for the faith which He has given us to believe on His name.

Chapter Four

At the beginning of the fourth chapter in the first epistle to Timothy, Paul departs from the subject of choosing qualified pastors, bishops, and deacons for the church, and begins to discuss a particular danger that would arise in the latter times. We read 1 Timothy 4:1-5:

> *"Now the Spirit speaketh expressly, that in the latter times some shall depart from the faith, giving heed to seducing spirits, and doctrines of devils; Speaking lies in hypocrisy; having their conscience seared with a hot iron; Forbidding to marry, and commanding to abstain from meats, which God hath created to be received with thanksgiving of them which believe and know the truth. For every creature of God is good, and nothing to be refused, if it be received with thanksgiving: For it is sanctified by the word of God and prayer."*

Concerning the phrase "latter times," I refer to the footnote in the *Pilgrim Bible*, which says: *"The latter days, or latter times, always refer to the last days of the age before Christ comes to reign."*

Before we begin our detailed study of these seducing spirits which Paul warns will infest the world during the latter times, I would like to first lay a scriptural foundation concerning the times that will precede the return of Christ. I know there are many of you who are confused about the second coming of Christ. You may hear from some preachers that the only reason that Christ is coming back to the earth is to destroy it and judge the dead. Then you hear us declaring that Christ is coming back to the earth to rule over the nations for one thousand years from His throne in Jerusalem. Those who say that Christ is not coming back to the earth contend that all the prophecies of which Jesus spoke were fulfilled when Jerusalem was destroyed in A.D. 70, or have been progressively fulfilled during the dispensation of grace. Many simply do not know what to believe.

For example, we have heard ministers ridicule the idea that Jesus would ever come back to the earth to reign. These ministers seem to have their scriptures and historical facts all in order and really present a strong case for A-millennialism. Anyone who is not an astute student of the Scriptures, and who is not able to rightly divide the Word could be misled. However, these A-millennialists are wrong. They refer only to those scriptures which seem to support their doctrine and thus, they willfully and knowingly distort the Scriptures. They contend that all of the prophecies have been fulfilled with the exception of one, that being the literal destruction of the world. They infer that no one can know when this will occur. The ministers who expound this doctrine are aptly described in 2 Peter 3:3-5, *"Knowing this first, that there shall come in the last days scoffers, walking after their own lusts, And saying, Where is the promise of his coming? for since the fathers fell asleep, all things continue as they were from the beginning of the creation. For this they willingly are ignorant of. . . ."*

In 2 Peter 1:19-21, Peter states that the main purpose of prophecy is so we will know when Christ's second coming is near. This is how these "scoffers" explain away the prophecies our Lord made in the Olivet Discourse: they say that all of these prophecies were fulfilled in that generation when Titus laid siege to Jerusalem and finally destroyed it. We believe that Josephus gave an accurate account of what happened during the siege of Jerusalem, and certainly all of the signs that Jesus gave in the Olivet Discourse were present. There is, however, a glaring error in the A-millennial argument; Jesus did not come back as He said He would. When Jesus began His ministry of three and a half years, He knew that Israel would not accept Him as the Messiah, the one who would fulfill the covenants made with the fathers concerning an earthly kingdom. Yet He was legally bound to give them every sign that He was the Messiah. He said, *". . . I am not sent but unto the lost sheep of the house of Israel"* (Matt. 15:24). Paul stated explicitly that Jesus came to Israel to confirm the covenants, yet throughout His ministry Jesus spoke of His rejection and death. The same is true of what happened at Jerusalem in A.D. 69 and A.D. 70. God gave Israel every indication that if they would repent and ask God to send Jesus back, Jesus' second coming would have been at that time. This is what Peter had preached to Israel in the first ten chapters of Acts. For example, we read in Acts 3:19-20, *"Repent ye therefore, and be converted, that your sins may be blotted out, when the times of refreshing shall come from the presence of the Lord; And he shall send Jesus Christ, which before was preached unto you."*

The A-millennialist contends that the abomination in the Temple which Christ spoke of occurred in A.D. 70, yet Paul spoke of this same event in 2 Thessalonians 2:3-4, *"Let no man deceive you by any means: for that day shall not come, except there come a falling away first, and that man of sin be revealed, the son of perdition; Who opposeth and exalteth himself above all that is called God, or that is worshipped; so that he as God sitteth in the temple of God, shewing himself that he is God."* Paul is referring here to the Antichrist, the world ruler, actually sitting in the Temple in Jerusalem claiming to be God. Now, this was not fulfilled in A.D. 70. The emperor of Rome at that time was Vespasian, the father of General Titus, and Vespasian was in Rome, not Jerusalem. Even Titus did not enter the Temple, because the Roman garrison broke through the wall and burned it to the ground.

Those of A-millennial persuasion contend that Christ is coming back for just one purpose — to destroy the world. The Book of Revelation was written in A.D. 96, twenty-six years after Jerusalem was destroyed. We read in Revelation 11:18 that Jesus is coming back to *". . . destroy them which destroy the earth."* So, Jesus is coming to save the earth from destruction, not destroy it.

The greatest evidence that Jesus is coming to reign on the earth is the refounding of Israel as a nation. In prophecy it is told how Israel would be scattered into all nations and then be regathered and the house of David restored. Even those Jews who are still blinded in Israel are today looking forward to the messianic age; and even these blinded Jews have more light than those who believe that Christ will not come back to reign over the earth. The prophecy to which Paul refers in 1 Timothy 4:1 was to be fulfilled in the "latter times," meaning just before Christ returns. We look over the world today and see the rise of spiritualism, astrology, ESP, mediums talking with the dead, ministers holding seances, devil worship, witchcraft, etc., and we know that we must be living in the latter times. Never has there been such a worldwide revival of spiritualism, even in the Dark Ages.

The word for seducing spirits in the Greek text is *planos*, meaning spirits from the outer darkness, roving spirits, spirits not of this world. Is it really true that today there are people who are talking with, and having intercourse with spirits from someplace other than the earth? For the answer, I will refer to Rev. Victor H. Ernest, who is a conservative Baptist minister of wide reputation. Before his call to the ministry, Rev. Ernest was a medium. I quote from the preface of his book, *I Talked With Spirits*:

> *"My primary object in writing this book is to demonstrate the reality and powers of evil spirits. I want to share how I became involved in communication with evil spirits, how these spirits — both appealing and loathsome — enslaved me, and how Jesus Christ set me free. This is primarily a personal testimony, not a comprehensive treatise on spirit phenomena. I am describing what I know by firsthand experience and the guidance of the Word of God. Spiritualism is very attractive because it promises knowledge of the future and communication with dead loved ones. Many people will be influenced by demonic spirits in this way without realizing it. The late Episcopalian bishop, James Pike, and the famous seeress Jeane Dixon, are two such people. The only sure guide into the shadowy spirit world is the Bible, and we neglect it at the peril of our souls. We do well to heed this statement by the noted spiritualist, Dr. Thomas Jay Hudson in his book* The Law Of Psychic Phenomena: *'The man who denies the*

phenomena of spiritism today is not entitled to be called a skeptic, he is simply ignorant.'
"

How do people get involved with evil spirits? Once again, I quote from Rev. Ernest's book:

"I could hardly wait for the next seance to take place so I could talk to my departed sister. . . . Six more days seemed like an eternity. I had no doubt that Iris would be present, though we had failed on the first attempt. I had talked with the spirit world many times in my twenty-one years, just as I talk with anyone else. I had listened to the spirits give lectures, sermons, exhortations, and counsel to the group assembled at our home seances. But I had never tried to talk to a dead person. My family, especially my mother's relatives, had been involved with spiritualism for several generations. They came to the United States from Holland before the Spanish-American War. On June 16, 1933, my seven-year-old sister died, and soon afterward a family from nearby Bemidji, Minnesota told us they had contacted the spirit of my dead sister and she was eager to talk to us. There were perhaps ten people gathered in the home for the seance. It didn't seem strange to us to open the seance by

saying the Lord's Prayer. We even ended '. . . in the name of the Father, Son, and Holy Spirit.' A prayer for a seance was offered and we sang familiar church hymns. . . . While we were singing, the medium slumped into unconsciousness, and before long a strange voice spoke through the medium's lips; it was a control spirit. . . . The spirit said that a family was present whose departed loved one wanted very much to speak with them but since she had been in the spirit world so short a time she was still adjusting to her new spiritual dimension and would communicate the following week. . . . At the second meeting we encountered another phase of spiritualism, the trumpet seance. When the medium entered his trance, the trumpet rose slowly from the table and dipped into a horizontal position. Eerily, it began spinning with a soft whir and moved around the room, stopping at intervals in midair. I sat rigid in amazement. I saw the floating trumpet, but I could not believe it. The trumpet went first to my mother, and then to other members of our family. And we heard a voice, supposedly my departed sister's. . . . Then the trumpet came to me. My first reaction was to grab it, and I snatched at the mouthpiece, but it darted away with amazing swiftness. I tried again, but it moved faster than I did. The trumpet finally settled directly in front of me, just out of my reach. Then the control spirit launched into a lecture about my non-belief, speaking through the unconscious medium. . . . As my emotions subsided, the trumpet hovered closer and closer to me until it was near my ear, its tip stroking my hair in the way my sister used to comb it.

"At later seances an older sister and I were told we could become gifted spirit mediums, and in time be able to contact the spirits in our own home. This sister and I began to practice the peace of passivity for five, six, then seven minutes, adding one minute each time. During these periods we tried to blot out every conscious thought from our minds. Eventually we could sit for fifteen and twenty-minute periods without being distracted by a single conscious thought. In one of the longer periods, the phenomenon finally took place that we had been waiting for. I witnessed the spirit taking control of my sister as she lost consciousness and a voice completely foreign to her soft contralto boomed out: 'My child, be not afraid. You have done well. Greater things than these you will do if you only believe. Continue in this way, and the marvels of the spirit world will be revealed to you.'

With that the spirit departed and sister regained consciousness. She asked what had happened, and I told her the words of the spirit. She was thrilled! . . . From that time on we held seances in our home for other people, with my young sister as the gifted medium.

"Some people say this is all a hoax, that spirits do not talk with human beings and floating objects are mere trickery. I would agree that a great many of the eerie demonstrations we hear about are clever illusions, but I believe on the basis of personal experience and the plain words of Scripture that spirits of the invisible world do communicate with humanity and do wield supernatural power in our visible world. And the ominous truth is that these spirits are not from God, but are fallen angels controlled by Satan. Their unholy mission is to lead human beings — by refined or gross means — away from dependence on God, their Creator, and they are active in spiritualist churches, seances, psychic phenomena, witchcraft, and idol worship. Individuals and nations who reject God, no matter how educated and prosperous they are, fall prey to the other god, Satan."

Thus we read the testimony of a man who worked

as a medium before he was converted to Christ and became a faithful minister of the gospel.

Let us read again 1 Timothy 4:1-2, *"Now the Spirit speaketh expressly, that in the latter times some shall depart from the faith, giving heed to seducing spirits, and doctrines of devils; Speaking lies in hypocrisy; having their conscience seared with a hot iron."* As we mentioned earlier, seducing spirits in the Greek is *planos*, spirits from other planets, the sanctuaries of Satan in the heavens spoken of in the Scriptures. I again quote from *I Talked With Spirits* by Rev. Ernest:

> *"I want to share some of the astounding things that took place in the living room of our Minnesota home. Here I experienced the six seances of spiritualism, passivity, vocal reality, trumpet revelation, lights, transfiguration, and levitation. Sometimes the spirit messages came to us in other languages. I remember Spanish, German, French, and the language of the Chippewa Indians being spoken. When we did not recognize the language the control spirit would tell us what it was and would interpret the central message. It often went something like this: 'Jesus is coming soon. He is even now at the threshold of the parapet of the heavenlies awaiting the word of the great spirit of lights. Wherefore, comfort ye one*

another with these words, and be ye ready;
for ye know not what hour he will come.'
When I asked the spirit how we could be
ready, the answer was always, 'Live a good
life, my child. Follow in the steps of the
master, the greatest medium of all.' This was
a vague reference to Jesus, without instructing us in what those steps were."

"When a medium went into a trance for
any length of time, his or her body became
very tired, causing the medium to spend a
day or two in bed after the seance. A most
striking phenomenon was a seance of vocal
reality I witnessed in connection with my
deceased great-grandfather and grandfather.
Both had been in the Spanish-American
War; one was a fifer and the other a
drummer. During the seance we heard feet
marching in perfect cadence, the music of a
fife, and the beat of drums. Each time, the
music was a popular tune of the times, 'The
Girl Left Behind Me.' I do not know how all
these sound vibrations could be distinctly
produced through the vocal apparatus of the
medium. In the seance of transfiguration,
the transfigured form of a loved one who has
died appears. A pastor friend of mine went
to a seance where his deceased mother
seemed to appear, clothed with light. She
drifted across the room to her son, stopped,

*and gave him a gentle smile. My friend
impetuously shouted 'Mother!' and leaped
up to embrace her, only to have her
disappear."*

I interrupt here to point out that what Rev.
Ernest is relating here about his experience as a
medium is according to the Bible. We remember that
Saul went to the witch of Endor and she brought up
Samuel with the aid of a familiar spirit. Quoting Rev.
Ernest again:

*"Little is known about the seance of levita-
tion. It was practiced only on a limited scale
in the seances I attended. Levitation is
sometimes called 'soul travel,' the phenomenon of spirit development whereby a medium
or an advanced convert to spiritualism can
leave his body by complete yieldedness to a
control spirit. He is not completely disunited
from his body, but is able to take conscious
flight from it to distant places. I experienced
this only once; I was taken into the spirit
dimension and witnessed indescribable
beauties. It's something I don't talk about."*

Rev. Ernest relates in his book that as he
progressed up the planes of spiritism, that he
remembers his mother once contradicting one of the
spirits from the Bible, so out of curiosity, he decided

to get a Bible. I again quote from his book:

> "*I had often wished that I had asked my mother what the spirit said to provoke her contradiction. Early in my life she had taught me things about God's existence, creation, and power. . . . Since I couldn't find a Bible in any store in our area, I wrote to Montgomery Wards for one. . . . I began to read in Genesis. . . . The first epistle of John was the first book I read in its entirety. When I got to the fourth chapter I read with amazement: 'Beloved, believe not every spirit, but try the spirits. . . .' This was just what I wanted. This must mean there were good spirits and bad spirits. I read on '. . . whether they are of God: because many false prophets are gone out into the world. Hereby know ye the Spirit of God: every spirit that confesseth that Jesus Christ is come in the flesh is of God; and every spirit that confesseth not that Jesus Christ is come in the flesh is not of God; and this is the spirit of antichrist, whereof ye have heard that it should come; and even now is it in the world.' I concluded from this that Jesus had come in the flesh to be a Savior, and that if I didn't believe this, I was wrong. I decided at the next seance I attended I would 'try the spirits' although I didn't know how to go about it. . . . I directed*

directed my first question to the control spirit. In fear and trembling, I asked if he believed that Jesus was the Son of God. I was so excited that it seemed someone else was asking the question. The control spirit answered smoothly, 'Of course, my child, Jesus is the Son of God. Only believe as the Bible says.' . . . Before long the trumpet was back to me, and I had to ask a second question. Since we were allowed only three questions, I was anxious to make mine count. This time I falteringly asked, 'O thou great and infinite spirit, do you believe that Jesus is the Savior of the world?' Almost before my words were uttered, the answer came: 'My child, why do you doubt? Why do you not believe? You have been this long time with us; why do you continue to doubt?' . . . When the trumpet returned for my third and last question, I reviewed what the spirit had said, and asked, 'O spirit, you believe that Jesus is the Son of God, that He is the Savior of the world — do you believe that Jesus died on the cross and shed His blood for the remission of sin?'

"The medium, deep in a trance, was catapulted off his chair. He fell in the middle of the living room floor and lay groaning as if in deep pain. The turbulent sounds suggested spirits in a carnival of confusion. We *all rushed forward to help him. The control spirit had prepared us with instructions about how to revive a person who had fainted. I never went to another seance. I had tested the spirits and found they were not of God. What I had thought to be a great power of God, the utopia of religious experience, had burst like a bubble. I realized that I had been in contact with the counterfeit of what God has to offer — and I wanted His reality. From that time I began to search God's Word to find the truth. In my early study of the Bible I had no difficulty believing in God, but I soon saw that to believe in God was not enough. Jesus had said, 'Believe also in me' (John 14:1). To believe in God as Creator was one thing; to believe in Jesus as the Savior was another, especially when he had to be my personal Savior. The first time I heard my voice calling to God I was frightened, but I kept at it and repeated my words to God several times. Showing my need to God, I said, 'Lord, I'm going to stay on my knees until I have the assurance that you have heard me and saved my soul.' Finally a great peace came into my heart, and I thanked the Lord that he heard me, received me, and saved me."*

The reference in 1 Timothy 4:1-3 to speaking lies

in hypocrisy refers to hypocrites within the church who turn from the faith to preach the doctrines of the devil. The hot iron referred to here by Paul is not an iron with which you ladies iron your husband's shirts. In Paul's day, slaves were branded by their masters with a hot iron much like the branding iron that ranchers use to brand their cattle. This is where the practice came from — the branding of slaves on the forehead, on the arm, or on some other part of their bodies. The reference to the searing of the conscience with a branding iron by Satan relates to the will to do his bidding — they have now become his servants.

Once again I quote from the book, *I Talked With Spirits:*

> *"Many people think that spirit phenomena are accomplished by trickery, sleight of hand, or black magic. I agree that many mysterious happenings associated with prominent psychics and small-town fortune-tellers are hoaxes — perhaps eighty-five percent of them, but I believe the rest are actual deeds of evil spirits counterfeiting the power of the Holy Spirit. At one trumpet seance, to prove there was no hocus-pocus involved, the control spirit sent the trumpet sailing between the rungs of the chair on which I was sitting. Since I was in my own home, I knew no props had been arranged and that no strings were attached. Who are*

the spirits that attend seances? Are they spirits of deceased people, as they claim? The Bible teaches that the spirits of the departed dead do not become either angels or demons spirits. These spirits are either with the Lord, waiting for the day of resurrection of their bodies (1 Thess. 4:14-17), or they are in Hell. There is much evidence in Scripture that the spirits who appear at seances are rebel angels. Jude 6 speaks about 'angels which kept not their first estate.' Many Bible scholars interpret Ezekiel 28:17, 'I will cast thee to the ground,' as indicating that the earth is the realm of Satan's powerful operations, with the help of his fallen colleagues, the demons. Satan is called the 'god of this world' in 2 Corinthians 4:4. And Christians are under attack by 'rulers . . . powers . . . world forces of darkness' (Eph. 6:12). God tells us that Hell was 'created for the devil and his angels (demons)' (Matt. 24:41). I was never told by the spirits who sent them, but as they oppose the truth that Jesus is the Savior from sin, it is obvious that they serve the master of sin, Satan. They are like the people in Jesus' day who rejected Him, and Jesus bluntly told them: 'Ye are of your father, the devil' (John 8:44). It is important to realize that the spirit world exists as another dimension all around us,

*not in some far-off place. The Bible speaks
of familiar spirits in 15 different places. For
example, we read in Isaiah 8:19, 22, 'And
when they shall say unto you, Seek unto
them that have familiar spirits, and unto
wizards that peep, and that mutter: should
not a people seek unto their God? for the
living to the dead? . . . And they shall look
unto the earth; and behold trouble and
darkness, dimness of anguish; and they shall
be driven to darkness.'*

*"When the medium at a seance enters
into a trance, a control spirit takes over and
allegedly introduces the spirit of a dead
person. In reality, the unseen visitor is a
'familiar spirit' who intimately knows the
dead person. Apparently these familiar spirits
accompany a person throughout life, becoming so well acquainted that they can con-
vincingly imitate the dead person's man-
nerisms and knowledge of personal details
when called upon at a seance. In this way
even close relatives are tricked into believing
they are hearing their dead loved one. I
believe that this was what happened to the
late James A. Pike. He went to several
mediums who told him they had contacted
his dead son, Jim, Jr., and that father and
son could communicate in a seance. Pike
supposedly did so on a number of occasions,*

as he describes in his book, The Other Side. *Actually, Pike talked to a spirit who was familiar with his son. This spirit impersonated his son so well and favorably that Pike overcame his remorse about his son's suicide, and looked forward to rejoining his son. Bishop Pike was a rather easy convert to spiritualism, since he, like the spiritualists, rejected the Christian doctrine of the Trinity, and if Jesus is not God, he cannot be man's Savior — nor does man need a Savior, in Pike's view.*

"Pike's third wife, Diane, was a secretary in a Methodist church before she married Pike. Her Christian beliefs were shallow also, as revealed in her book, Search. *She describes a vision given her while her husband was dying in the Israeli wilderness. She confesses: 'The strangest part for me was to see so literally what I had supposed to be a symbolic expression of meaning.' Diane Pike, and hundreds of thousands of other people, have difficulty believing the extraordinary claims of the Bible, yet they unhesitatingly accept the vagaries of personal fancy or the mysterious manifestation of spirits. This reminds us of the prophecy in 1 Timothy 4:1 about 'giving heed to seducing spirits, and doctrines of demons. . . .'"*

In the November 1970 edition of the *Ladies*

Home Journal, Bishop Pike's widow relates certain attempts by Pike since his death to contact her. These attempts described by her correspond with the activities of familiar spirits as described by Rev. Ernest. I quote from the article:

"In several of my early experiences of apparent communications with Jim, he seemed to be trying to express his love and concern. . . . But I was aware that something was different. Although Jim seemed to receive my embrace with warmth and love in it, he did not return it. . . . It was as though Jim had waited to come back to me until I had had an opportunity to see that I could get along without him. It was like a trial period. . . . And even though Jim had appeared to me physically — so much so that touching the back of his head and his hair made such a vivid impression on me that I could still feel it on my left hand for days afterward — he did not relate to me physically. He could understand me, but he could not be physical with me anymore. . . . There was no wish for fulfillment of recreation of our past relationship. This added to my feeling that Jim 'came back' to me by ESP or some other means. . . . The first real request I made of Jim was prompted by the death of the twenty-one-year-old son of some friends of

*ours. I went into meditation then, telling Jim
that Russ had died and asking him to be
there to help Russ over to the other side.
After nearly an hour, I knew Jim's response:
He knew Russ had died, but somehow it was
not his role or function to receive him.
Others would, however, and once Russ
made the original adjustment to 'the other
side,' Jim would be able to be in contact with
him. The message was as clear to me as if I
had called Jim on the telephone."*

The widow of James Pike continues to parrot the
patented rhetoric of the mediums who supposedly
commune through familiar spirits with the dead. In
his lifetime Bishop Pike denied the Divine inspiration
of the Scriptures, the Genesis account of creation, the
virgin birth of Christ, and the blood atonement. His
widow now places her hope on life after death for her
husband, not on his personal faith in Christ as Savior,
but rather on her contact with him through the spirits,
which according to Rev. Ernest, who has talked at
length with spirits, contends that it is the familiar
spirit of Pike who is now imitating him.

Rev. Ernest comments on another proponent of
spiritual powers, and we quote:

*"In claiming these powers, mediums and
psychics turn people away from God's source
of revelation and guidance, the holy*

Scriptures. The famous Jeane Dixon claims her gift of prophecy and visions are from God, but she also says in Gift Of Prophecy *that the same Almighty Power is guiding all people, whatever their religion. She apparently does not consider the possibility that her supernatural gift could come from Satan rather than from God. . . . Rather than contacting spirits while in a trance, Jeane speaks of 'vibrations' that transmit knowledge to her about other people and future events. This is a power mentioned by some Satan worshippers and fortune-tellers. The scriptural 'gift of prophecy,' in contrast with Mrs. Dixon's, emphasized righteous conduct in connection with predictions about future events. Mrs. Dixon does use her gift unselfishly, but she does not use her gift to teach people about God's righteousness. Jeane Dixon's understanding of the Bible and God's will seems seriously deficient. In* Gift Of Prophecy, *she says: 'Once you have visions like that . . . you know what it is to truly worship God. . . . But this does not mean that you can dump your problems on the Lord without effort on your own part. I get very annoyed with men of the cloth who tell their flock to give their problems to the Lord. God gave us our own work to do.' This self-dependence (of which Jeane Dixon speaks) is the very sin that keeps millions of people from acknowledging they need a Savior from their sins — and someone who is able to handle the deep problems of life for them. No Christian has God's sanction to seek occult knowledge of future events, and any person who does so risks envelopment in Satan's silken net of spirit enslavement. Spirit inquiry and craving for the unknown is a denial of the adequacy and supremacy of God's written revelation to man. The Apostle Paul wrote that we 'walk by faith, not by sight' (2 Cor. 5:7)."*

In relation to the doctrines of devils, Paul says that some would forbid marriage and command the abstinence from meats. In Paul's day there was an ascetic Jewish brotherhood who lived on the shores of the Dead Sea called the Essenes. Membership was restricted to non-married males and they abstained from animal meat. The Gnostic apostasy also involved the eating of certain foods and abstinence from meat. Paul wrote the epistle to the church at Colosse to expose the spiritual evil that was in Gnosticism. We read in Colossians 2:16, *"Let no man therefore judge you in meat, or in drink, or in respect of an holyday, or of the new moon, or of the sabbath days."*

Of course, the Catholic Church incorporated some of these beliefs concerning celibacy for servants of the church and the abstinence from meats on certain occasions. It is entirely possible that Paul was referring to the Essenes, the Gnostics, or even in a prophetic sense to the doctrines of the Catholic Church. However, we must also consider strongly that he meant these strange practices to be related to the latter times as mentioned at the beginning of 1 Timothy 4. The type of food one eats plays an important part in spiritual development within the occult. Quoting once more Rev. Ernest:

"The spirits I encountered at seances were, for the most part, very moralistic. They encouraged us not to smoke or drink or do anything else that would harm our minds and bodies. Ministers were told to preach morality, good manners, and civic pride. I knew ministers who actually had spirit messages taken down by their secretaries and then used them from the pulpit! The spirits often talked about an ethical Jesus, but never about the Savior who died a sacrificial death for sin. In contrast to the high moral and ethical tone of the seances in our home, I attended some where the spirits were blasphemous and sensual. Spiritualists call them earth-bound demons, and they served to re-enforce our conviction that the spirits at our seances were truly from God. Only later did I realize that the blasphemous seances were another subtle trick of Satan to

> *convince us that there were 'good' spirits and*
> *'bad' spirits, and that we were indeed*
> *communicating with God at our seances.*
> *For all evil spirits are demons, fallen creatures*
> *serving Satan. Even the spirits who told us*
> *to improve ourselves morally and spiritually*
> *were doing so to gain our allegiance for*
> *themselves and keep us from God Himself.*
> *Even mediums are often unaware that they*
> *are dealing with the kingdom of Satan."*

The reference here to evil spirits dictating to ministers what to preach in their pulpit on Sunday makes literal the admonition of Paul in 2 Corinthians 11:13, 15, *"For such are false apostles, deceitful workers, transforming themselves into the apostles of Christ. Therefore it is no great thing if his ministers also be transformed as the ministers of righteousness; whose end shall be according to their works."*

No place in the Bible does God command celibacy or for a person to remain in a non-marital status. Paul does bring out in 1 Corinthians 7:25 that in some cases it is better for those in the Lord's service not to marry, but he leaves this decision up to the individual. We believe that Paul was married when he was a member of the Sanhedrin, and it is evident that his wife either died or divorced him. He did not remarry because it would have hindered his own particular work to which God had called him. However, God does not call us all to be a Paul. He calls some of us to be established pastors and in most cases it is preferable for pastors and church leaders to be settled, married men. What I believe Paul wrote about concerning marriage in relation to demon possession was a general breakdown in the family unit — discrediting the institution of marriage, and this we know is taking place in our day.

Today there are active spiritualists and passive spiritualists. Rev. Ernest brought out that in some instances the familiar spirit will actually dictate to the minister what to preach in church on Sunday, and according to the Apostle John, the true test of an evil spirit is that it will deny the virgin birth and the blood atonement of Christ. We look across the land today and what do we see — the pulpits filled with ministers of Satan denying the virgin birth and the blood atonement. Bishop Pike was such a minister until the death of his son drove him into active spiritualism. Concerning the command to abstain from meats, those who consort with familiar spirits and act as mediums never eat meat. The same rule applied to many of the prophets of God in the Old Testament. We remember that Daniel refused the king's meat and ate a vegetable diet. Spirit beings, the angels of God, actually communed with him. The same is true of communion with evil spirits — the eating of flesh drives them away. Rev. Victor Ernest, who was once a spiritualist medium himself, answers some of the most often asked questions about demons and evil spirits in his book. I would like to share this information with you. We quote Rev. Ernest:

Q. *Are there healing meetings in spiritualism?*

A. *Yes. Every seance group I have been familiar with has healing meetings. Usually the medium touches the affected areas, moves his hands down over the area of pain, then quickly removes them in a sweeping motion. This action is completed with a snap of the hands and wrists, as though the pain were actually being withdrawn. I have seen people helped temporarily, but not permanently. Just how far God has permitted Satan to extend himself in the area of healing, I cannot say.*

Q. *Do some people have more "magical" or spiritual powers than others?*

A. *We are all different, and therefore no two people respond the same way. I was taught by a spirit that my "soul force" would be greatly affected by what I did or did not eat. Mediums with strong powers are strict vegetarians (psychic Jeane Dixon eats almost no meat). Their main diet is celery, carrot juice, and fruit. We were taught in the seance that Adam and Eve were vegetarians.*

Q. *What is fire-walking as it is practiced in some parts of the world today?*

A. *For centuries, fire-walking has been considered a means of spiritual purification and authority. There are references to it in the Old Testament. The ancients in Canaan sought favor with their gods by walking on fiery hot stones. It is still practiced in* *secret religious rites among certain tribes in India and Africa. A fire-walker enters a trance before he starts across the hot coals. There is nothing fake about this — he literally walks on hot coals of fire, or sometimes, on a lava flow. Having finished the course, he is recognized as having been accepted by a god and having great spiritual powers.*

Q. *Is there any record in the Bible of direct competition between the power of God and the power of Satan?*

A. *Yes. The experience of Moses and Aaron with the magicians of Egypt (Exo. 7:8-12) is an example of this. When Aaron's rod was turned into a serpent, the magicians did likewise with theirs. But Aaron's serpent swallowed theirs, demonstrating God's sovereignty.*

Q. *Is there a spiritual reason why some dogs and cats shy away from some people but warm up to others?*

A. *I was told by a control spirit at a seance that every person gives forth a vibration that cannot only be be felt by some people with psychic powers, but which can be seen by animals. These psychic vibrations supposedly indicate a person's plane of spiritual development. Some spiritualists think they explain why some people are introverts, others extroverts. Extroverts, for example, are supposed to give off warm color shadows that can be seen by animals.*

A. *Do all spiritualists respect the Bible?*

Q. *Like all non-Christians, spiritualists respect the Bible as far as it is useful to them. Moses Hull* *claimed the Bible as the work of mediums. 1 Corinthians is considered the greatest spirit revelation of the Apostle Paul, where he said, "I know nothing by myself." Spiritualists interpret this to mean Paul had a mighty control spirit who revealed things to him.*

Q. *Is it possible for a person who is demon-possessed to confess Christ?*

A. *In Acts 16 the account is given of a young lady who followed Paul and Silas for many days, testifying that they were servants of the most high God who showed the people the way of salvation. Paul knew that she was doing this by Satan's instigation, and he finally rebuked the demon spirit speaking through the girl. It immediately left her. Mark's gospel tells of a man indwelt with an unclean spirit, who cried out, "What have I to do with thee, Jesus, thou Son of the most high God?" Jesus rebuked the demons — they were many — and refused to accept their testimony. In both cases, we see that it was possible for people afflicted with demons to confess Christ.*

Q. *Do you think mental telepathy is a spiritualist phenomenon?*

A. *Mental telepathy is said to be the projection of thought by a mind dominated by suggestion. I believe it occurs when the mind gets in tune with a spirit force, or a control spirit, and is projected by a spirit being.*

Q. *What is the spirit world like?*

A. *I asked a spirit this question and got this answer: "It* *is filled with color. There are all colors whereby the individual is made happy." In the spirit world, the emotions of the soul are affected by color. There are only "happy colors" there, no pale, grey, dark, or depressing colors. Scientists are discovering the effect that colors have on a person's emotions. Some of this research is used in packaging merchandise. The effect of colors on the spirit is comparable to the effects of music on the emotions.*

Q. *How can we know that you have not made up some of your stories, since you do not name the persons involved?*

A. *First, my basic tenet is the Bible, the Word of God, which I have consistently referred to. Second, if anyone writes to me in care of the publisher, I will gladly document any point I have made. Third, I do not want to embarrass some people mentioned in this book, who are now delivered from spiritualism.*

In light of what Rev. Ernest has said about the effect of color and sound, we should keep in mind that Satan is the god of chaos and confusion. Everywhere we turn or go today, we hear a jumble of sounds and a jumble of colors and shapes. It is difficult for a man to find a peaceful atmosphere within which to meditate upon the truths of God. In this we see the attempt of the devil to keep men in a state of mental confusion and spiritual frustration. Rev. Ernest has reproduced in his book a letter received from a spiritualist organization in Los Angeles called the Legion of

Lucifer, and it demonstrates the depth of satanic involvement of many who are attempting at this time to bring in the kingdom of the Antichrist. Now remember, this letter is from a satanic organization. Notice how they reverse the meaning of scriptures. The devil continues to produce his lies.

> *"Now we believe, we of the New Movement, that the great Prince Michael, mentioned in the eleventh and twelfth chapters of Daniel, is the Archangel Michael, who has foresworn allegiance to Jehovah, and is now on our side. We believe that Michael is the alter ego of Satan, or rather Lucifer, who takes on many names. First, let me explain that we have formed a movement which is necessarily secret for the time being — a militant organization. We call ourselves The Legion of Lucifer. Contrary to popular misconception and Christian propaganda, Lucifer was not and is not the ugly, cruel entity he is so often portrayed to be; but on the contrary, he is the most beautiful, intelligent, resplendent of all the cherubs of heaven, that is, prior to the revolution against Jehovah, who feared his growing power and dominion. . . . The antichrist will eventually rule the world. That, too, you have envisioned; and the antichrist, the archangel Michael, and Lucifer are all one and the same, in a trinity. . . .*

That Armageddon is close at hand is, I think, easy for anyone to see, and the unleashing of the atomic bomb points to the inevitable conclusion. The atomic bomb, I am glad, is of satanic origin, a product of the infernal. . . . The hosts and cohorts of heaven must fall before Lucifer's ultimate assault. You will recall that in the contest between Jesus and Satan, Jesus, the younger Son of God, was given a chance by his elder brother, Lucifer, or Satan, to share his dominion, but he chose to become an opponent rather than be second-in-command to his elder brother. At that time, Lucifer simply departed from him for a season and has been biding his time, content to see what a mess Jesus and his followers were to make of the world and humanity. Jesus and Christiantiy have, I think, demonstrated their weakness and inability to cope with the opinions and the minds of men, and we are now worse off and in more disharmony over the globe than in any previous period of history. The kingdom of Lucifer is nigh, and we, The Legion of Lucifer, have pledged ourselves to it, and the reign of Jesus or his attempt to reign is collapsing on every side."

This is all of the letter from the Legion of Lucifer that Rev. Ernest included in his book that I will quote, and the reason I included the part that I did was to give you an idea of the doctrine and dedication of the devil cults that are rising up in our day, a part of the end-time picture that Paul describes in 1 Timothy 4. Now, some may conclude that this is pretty far out — devil worshippers, witches, mediums, familiar spirits, demon possession are just too much to stomach in this enlightened scientific age. And indeed, we were told that science was going to erase all superstition concerning demons, spirits, and angels from the world. But look what has happened. There has been a revival of witchcraft unprecedented in all history. Cities are even appointing official witches. Horoscopes are appearing in over two thousand daily newspapers. Devil worship is becoming popular. ESP, fortune-telling, and seances are the rage of the day.

We are discussing spiritual seduction, and Paul says in 1 Timothy 4:3 that this deception would occur also in forbidding of meats. Those who consort with familiar spirits seldom eat meat, and they observe a rigid set of rules whereby they might evolve to such a high spiritual plane that they become immortal. We are informed in the Scriptures that Satan holds the power of death, and this was part of the lie with which he deceived Eve. ". . . *Ye shall not surely die*" (Gen. 3:4).

The only person I have known who professed to be a Christian and who turned away and became involved with spiritism was Dr. James Hollenbeck. I have made mention of him before. He was a well-educated man, a world traveler, and a noted archaeologist. Our founder, E.F. Webber, was alive when Dr. Hollenbeck appeared on our broadcast several times. He seemed to be a dedicated man of God. In the early 1960s, he got involved in spiritualism and believed he was evolving up the spiritual place to the point where he believed he would never die. He claimed he could be in Los Angeles and send his spirit to New York City. It was only a few months later that an article appeared in our local paper stating that Dr. Hollenbeck had died under mysterious circumstances in his hotel room. All the windows and doors were locked from the inside, and the police have never solved the mystery.

> *"If thou put the brethren in remembrance of these things, thou shalt be a good minister of Jesus Christ, nourished up in the words of faith and of good doctrine, whereunto thou hast attained"* (1 Tim. 4:6).

Paul reminded Timothy that it is the duty of every minister to remind the Christians of the warfare that exists in the spiritual realm between God and the devil. The reason that so many people today are becoming involved in spiritualism and the occult is that preachers are silent on the subject. They have been brainwashed into believing that it is superstition to believe in a personal devil or warn the congregation about evil spirits.

"But refuse profane and old wives' fables, and exercise thyself rather unto godliness. For bodily exercise profiteth little: but godliness is profitable unto all things, having promise of the life that now is, and of that which is to come" (1 Tim. 4:6-8).

Profane is exactly the opposite meaning of godliness. Profane means unholy, unhallowed, dirty, evil — that which emanates from the pit of Hell. Paul says reject it — get away from it — cast it out. We live in a profane world. Profane literature fills our mailboxes, profane language beats against our ears, and even little children watch profane television programs. It is difficult to reject the profane and the evil spiritualism of our day, because it is continually before our eyes and beating against our ears. It would be well for us to consider Paul's advice in regard to spiritual exercise. The apostle first says that bodily exercise profits little. Now we know that he certainly did not mean that exercise was not good for the body, because it is. Exercise helps to keep our body strong and enables us to resist the strains and diseases that continually buffet the flesh. And inasmuch as we should exercise to keep our body strong, even more so should we indulge in continual spiritual exercise to be able to resist the enemies of our souls, meaning the devil and his angels. Bodily exercise will profit only for a little while — meaning as long as our bodies last. But spiritual exercise will be of benefit to us for eternity, because by keeping ourselves built-up in the faith the devil will not be able to rob us of our eternal rewards to be given at the Judgment Seat of Christ. This was what Paul meant in Ephesians 6:10-12: *"Finally, my brethren, be strong in the Lord, and in the power of his might. Put on the whole armour of God, that ye may be able to stand against the wiles of the devil. For we wrestle not against flesh and blood, but against principalities, against powers, against the rulers of the darkness of this world, against spiritual wickedness in high places."*

Just as a wrestler gets into a ring and pits his physical strength against an opponent, Paul says we are daily pitted in spiritual combat with the forces of the devil, and unless we keep ourselves spiritually strong, we will lose the contest. Quoting Rev. Victor Ernest from his book, *I Talked With Spirits*:

"Satan's campaign has always been as virulent against God's people as against people without faith. Since Satan cannot attack God directly, he attacks God through Christians. Whenever God's people fail to serve Him faithfully, Satan rejoices in his victories. Many Christians are 'devoured' by worldly interests that distract them from spiritual service to God. . . . Satan schemes to devour Christians by sensuality. He is alert to tempt men and women, single and married, pastors and laymen, into sinful

relationships that will ruin families and careers and defame the name of Christ. Christians who fail to grow in their faith are easy targets for Satan. Unprepared for Satan's snares and signals, they have little defense against his suggestions to their mind. . . . In view of the mighty impact that satanic forces are making upon contemporary life, and recognizing the decline of spiritual vigor within our churches, I am convinced that we must return to the protracted church meetings of two generations ago for a counterattack on the cancerous indifference poisoning the body of Christ. Holy Spirit-filled evangelists and gospel singers are needed to hold extended meetings and declare the precious gospel that is able to save 'from the gutter-most to the uttermost' and to storm the spiritual citadels of Satan erected within the Christian fellowship. Christians everywhere must be willing to leave their favorite TV programs and their weekend holidays to get back spiritually where God can use us to prove to this generation that 'greater is he' that is in us than he that is betraying the world."

We now read 1 Timothy 4:9-10:

"This is a faithful saying and worthy of all

acceptation. For therefore we both labour and suffer reproach, because we trust in the living God, who is the Saviour of all men, specially of those that believe."

Again, we note that the Greek word for faithful saying means something that we can accept as an absolute truth, something like a rock that we can stand on, a cornerstone of the church. The state religion of Rome at that time was Caesar worship which demanded the recognition of the emperor as the chief benefactor of all mankind — the one from whom all blessings flowed throughout the then-known world. But Paul presented Jesus Christ as the Savior "of all men," meaning mankind — especially those who would believe on His name unto everlasting life.

"These things command and teach. Let no man despise thy youth; but be thou an example of the believers, in word, in conversation, in charity, in spirit, in faith, in purity. Till I come, give attendance to reading, to exhortation, to doctrine. Neglect not the gift that is in thee, which was given thee by prophecy, with the laying on of the hands of the presbytery. Meditate upon these things; give thyself wholly to them; that thy profiting may appear to all. Take heed unto thyself, and unto the doctrine; continue in them: for

*in doing this thou shalt both save thyself,
and them that hear thee"* (1 Tim. 4:11-16).

In these closing verses of this chapter, Paul admonishes Timothy not to let others in the church at Ephesus despise, that is reject him or attempt to discredit him because of his youth. Of course, Timothy was not in reality a young man at that time. He was really middle-aged, being forty years old. However, he was young in comparison to Paul and the presbytery of the church. We see revealed here a hint of backbiting in the church, which occurred even in the early churches. Some thought that one of the older men should be the minister, so Paul admonished Timothy to keep studying and to bring messages that were based on love, faith, and godliness, and he would remain above reproach. The presbytery originally referred to a select group of the eldest members of the Sanhedrin, and Paul borrowed the term to apply to the elders of the church. The apostle reminds Timothy of his responsibility to those who ordained him to the ministry and appointed him bishop over the church which he pastored.

In conclusion of this thought, Paul declares that if Timothy would keep himself grounded in the faith and continue to expound sound doctrine, he would "save" himself and those who sat under his ministry. Now, Paul was not referring to soul salvation. Let us go back to the beginning of the chapter, *"Now the Spirit speaketh expressly, that in the latter times some shall depart from the faith, giving heed to seducing spirits, and doctrines of devils."* Why would they depart from the faith? Because they would heap to themselves false teachers who would tickle their ears and build them up in their own vanity. But, Paul tells Timothy that if he will keep well grounded in the faith and teach likewise, then he and the members of his congregation will be saved from spiritual intercourse with familiar, or seducing spirits. The Bible is filled with examples of men who failed to yield themselves completely to the will of God and the leading of the blessed Holy Spirit. They wanted to retain a measure of self-control themselves, and to such men, the devil presents a daily challenge. It is difficult for any of us to empty our body and soul of all self and be filled completely with Christ. We must be on guard constantly against false prophets and false spirits. We must always be diligent to try the spirits and prove whether they are of God or Satan. Rev. Victor Ernest, in the closing chapter of his book, provides us with this summary which is certainly worthy of our consideration:

1. *The fact that a phenomenon is spiritual does not necessarily mean it is an act of God.*
2. *The true character of spirits can be exposed by their rejection of Jesus Christ as God the Son who died to atone for mankind's sin.*
3. *A familiar spirit in the service of Satan knows human beings so well that he can disguise himself as*

those people.

4. *There are different kinds of spirits (Mark 9:29) — some are sensual and lewd, and others appear ethical.*

5. *Demons are wandering spirits belonging to the legions of Satan, a class of beings distinct from angels — some are on earth seeking embodiment in human beings and animals, others already are imprisoned in the bottomless abyss.*

6. *God has forbidden humans to try to communicate with the departed dead; such attempts result in communication with deceitful spirits, known as 'familiar' spirits.*

7. *Satan wins, followed by psychic and supernatural phenomena that approximate the power of God.*

8. *Satan is a created being who presently exercises authority over his domain, the earth realm, but he can do only what God allows him to do, and eventually he will be deprived of all power and glory.*

9. *Satan attacks at the Christian's vulnerable points, often where the Christian thinks he is strong and secure — only vigilance and spiritual armor will keep the Christian victorious.*

10. *Guardian angels protect the Christian from demonic assaults that God will not permit — the true Christian is securely on the winner's side!"*

Chapter Five

"Rebuke not an elder, but intreat him as a father; and the younger men as brethren; The elder women as mothers; the younger as sisters, with all purity" (1 Tim. 5:1-2).

In this scripture, Paul gives instructions concerning the Christian fellowship which God desires. He uses the family unit to illustrate the proper relationship of the various members of the church. We know that God has a family because we are so instructed in Ephesians 3:14-15, *"For this cause I bow my knees unto the Father of our Lord Jesus Christ, Of whom the whole family in heaven and earth is named."* A son of God is one who has been born into God's family through a special or direct creative act of God the Creator. Adam is called a son of God in Luke 3:38 because he was a direct creation of God. But before Adam, God had heavenly sons, the angels, as we read in Hebrews 1:4-14. Angels were created by God as spirit beings, and throughout the Scriptures they are called sons of God. However, from the human race there were no sons of God from Adam to the Lord Jesus Christ. But we know that God willed from before the foundation of the world to have an addition to His family from man to inherit heavenly places with Christ and be joint-heirs with His only begotten Son. The reason for this great and mighty beneficiency toward the redeemed from among men is not known. All we know is that He is a God of love and He has a plan and purpose for the universe that will be fulfilled. Perhaps the church is to fill the gap in Heaven left by the rebellion of Lucifer and the angels who followed him in the trangression. In any event, Christians have been translated into the family of God through the miracle of the new birth by faith in Jesus Christ. We read in 1 John 3:1, *"Behold, what manner of love the Father hath bestowed upon us, that we should be called the sons of God. . . ."*

This is the great truth to which Paul refers in 1 Timothy 5:1-2 — mainly that Christians belong to one big family and as members of this family their attitudes toward one another should be accordingly. An elder member of the church should be accepted as a father, those near your own age or younger as brothers and sisters, older women as mothers, and much younger members as sons and daughters. Paul thought of Timothy as his son in the faith. This universal family of God to which Christians belong will never be broken up by death or separation. After Christ returns, we will live together forever in the mansions which Jesus Christ is preparing for us. And in light of the fact that Christians will live forever together as a family in the heavens, Paul entreats us to learn to live together as brothers, sisters, mothers, and fathers within the church on earth. If all Christians could truly attain to this united spiritual relationship, then we could go out and win the world for Jesus.

This is the only type of ecumenism of which the Bible speaks. The ecumenism of our day in the uniting of the denominations for social causes is of the devil. Also, the universal fatherhood of God and brotherhood of man theory is an illusion. God is the father of those who belong to His family. You become a member of God's family only by being born into it by faith in Jesus Christ. Let us continue now and read 1 Timothy 5:3-16:

> *"Honour widows that are widows indeed. But if any widow have children or nephews, let them learn first to shew piety at home, and to requite their parents: for that is good and acceptable before God. Now she that is a widow indeed, and desolate, trusteth in God, and continueth in supplications and prayers night and day. But she that liveth in pleasure is dead while she liveth. And these things give in charge, that they may be blameless. But if any provide not for his own, and specially for those of his own house, he hath denied the faith, and is worse than an infidel. Let not a widow be taken into the number under threescore years old, having been the wife of one man, Well reported of for good works; if she have*

brought up children, if she have lodged strangers, if she have washed the saints' feet, if she have relieved the afflicted, if she have diligently followed every good work. But the younger widows refuse: for when they have begun to wax wanton against Christ, they will marry; Having damnation, because they have cast off their first faith. And withal they learn to be idle, wandering about from house to house; and not only idle, but tattlers also and busybodies, speaking things which they ought not. I will therefore that the younger women marry, bear children, guide the house, give none occasion to the adversary to speak reproachfully. For some are already turned aside after Satan. If any man or woman that believeth have widows, let them relieve them, and let not the church be charged; that it may relieve them that are widows indeed."

Prior to the fifth chapter, Paul has described the business of the church as maintaining order within, casting out those who are servants of Satan, contending for the faith, preaching the gospel, being diligent in the appointing of men grounded in the faith as pastors and deacons, and feeding the flock, while warning them always of the wiles of the devil.

Now we come to the social obligations of the church. And the social and charitable sphere of the church we find is extremely limited and to be carried on very carefully while observing the warnings given by the Apostle Paul. It would appear from Scripture that the social obligation assumed by the early churches was limited to taking care of the widows. We read in Acts 6:1-2, *"And in those days, when the number of the disciples was multiplied, there arose a murmuring of the Grecians against the Hebrews, because their widows were neglected in the daily ministration. Then the twelve called the multitude of the disciples unto them, and said, It is not reason that we should leave the word of God, and serve tables."*

In this instance, the Hellenist Jews, or the Alexandrian Jews, complained that the widows among them were neglected while the traditional Hebrew widows were well taken care of. We refer to this incident only to show more clearly that it was the custom for the church to feed the widows and their children. However, Paul gave the admonition to Timothy to honor, or help, those widows who were truly widows. In order for a widow to be deserving of help, we note that she should be desolate, without means of support, or even any near relative to help her. She should be godly with the graciousness to always be ready to help the church in any way she is called upon, in return for the charity the church has shown toward her (v. 10). Now we read in verse nine, *"Let not a widow be taken into the number under threescore years old, having been the wife of one man."* The phrase "taken into the number" in the

Greek means to place on a church roster, and in the sense it is used here, it evidently refers to a church roll for assistance. In other words, no widow under sixty years of age was to be considered eligible for permanent assistance from the church.

This does not mean that a younger widow could not be cared for on a temporary basis if she and her children were hungry, but Paul warns against creating a situation whereby Christians would be supporting and encouraging fornication. The reference to younger widows waxing wanton actually means giving in to lustful emotions, including fornication. Thus, should the church make a practice of supporting young widows, they would become content to accept church charity while not looking for husbands or gainful employment, and thereby increase their dependent children in number.

We see the wisdom of Paul's warning about establishing precedents that cannot be reversed. Today, Christians are taxed by the government to support women while they give birth to illegitimate children. In most states, the more illegitimate children they have, the more money they get. Thus, we have a never-ending cycle of encouraging more and more immorality through social programs that were originally intended for good. Paul says these women will grow lustful, greedy, and become tale-bearers — biting the hands that feed them. I think a good example of what has happened in the world appeared in an AP news release dated November 20, 1970, where a thirty-three-year-old female school teacher who made $11,000 the prior year, manipulated her earnings so she could draw $172 a month for her two children during the summer months. All over this nation, women are drawing dependent aid for illegitimate children and the percentage of illegitimate births continues to spiral upward every year.

In verse sixteen Paul says, *"If any man or woman that believeth have widows, let them relieve them, and let not the church be charged. . . ."* In other words, God puts the main responsibility for social work and charity upon the individual. In verse eight we read, *". . . if any provide not for his own, and specially for those of his own house, he hath denied the faith, and is worse than an infidel."* "Those of his own house" refers to wife and children, and this responsibility also extends to the sick and the widows within the family — mothers, fathers, sisters, brothers, etc. To delegate this responsibility to the nation is to create a welfare state that will eventually bankrupt and destroy the political and economic order, and make liars, thieves, and robbers of a growing segment of the population until it is impossible to sustain any form of representative government. To delegate this responsibility to the church will bring utter ruin and chaos to the congregations and denominations. I quote an article from *Christian Economics* entitled "Can the Church Be Saved?":

"The church which came into being was

intended as a channel of salvation, spiritual instruction, edification, and blessing to the world. Now, with a track record extending over two millennia, it develops that the church herself is in need of salvation. Having turned her back on Jesus Christ, abandoned the gospel and flouted the Word of God, a very large segment of the contemporary church has embarked on a humanistic binge and is so hopelessly lost at sea that she stands in need of salvation. To browse through a file of materials on the church today is like strolling through a horror-filled jungle. Item after item tells the sad story of a church wandering in apostasy. The church is taking an active part in the youth revolt. Obscene publications are rolling off the church presses. Political revolutions are being spawned in church institutions. Clergy-men are preaching and publishing sermons on far-out topics like 'The Advantages Of Adultery.' Secular magazines are coming out with articles which rebuke the church under titles like 'An Obituary For God.' . . . Our Judeo-Christian heritage, with its emphasis on property individualism, respon-sibility, and hard work, has been a major influence underlying the greatness of Western civilization. Humanism, on the other hand, dispenses with God and the will of God. It *attempts to cope with human problems by the effete and tragic method of substituting human wisdom for Divine guidance. . . . Great responsibility devolves upon Christian laymen today. None are so hopeless and remote from salvation as clergymen who, knowing better, have deliberately spurned Christ, the gospel, and the Word of God. Such men will continue their evil works and influences as long as laymen permit them to hold positions in the churches. Let sincere Christian laymen, in whom the power ultimately resides, begin now to assert themselves. Let them rise up with holy resolution and throw the apostate clergymen out of the church where they belong. A nationwide movement of this kind could accomplish nothing but good. It might even be the salvation of the church."*

Now isn't it strange? Paul said exactly the same thing almost two thousand years ago right here in his first epistle to Timothy. The reason the larger denominations today are lost in a sea of social, economic, and political causes is because they have not remained faithful to the ordinances for carrying on the business of the church which is, preaching the gospel and contending for the faith, as enumerated by the Apostle Paul in his pastoral epistles.

"Let the elders that rule well be counted

worthy of double honour, especially they who labour in the word and doctrine. For the scripture saith, Thou shalt not muzzle the ox that treadeth out the corn. And, The labourer is worthy of his reward" (1 Tim. 5:17-18).

The reference here to giving honor to an elder means a monetary reward for faithful Christian service. It is to be understood in the same sense that the church gave honor to needy widows. This means recognizing their worthiness to be assisted in a material way by the church. Often when a guest speaker appears on our broadcast, if he has gone to extra personal expense and a loss of salary elsewhere to be on the broadcast, we will give him an honorarium. The reference to the ox treading out the corn relates back to Deuteronomy 25:4. In those days, they didn't have modern thrashing machines like we do today. They would heap the grain crops in a circle and walk oxen over it until the grain had been separated from the stalk. It was considered cruelty to muzzle the animals while they were treading out the grain. Likewise, those in full-time Christian service are engaged in a harvest — the harvest of souls. Paul declares plainly that such servants of the Lord are entitled to receive earnings for themselves and their families from the church treasury. Often times, we receive mean and hateful letters accusing us of conducting a ministry only for the money that we receive in salary, but these accusers are to be pitied because they are woefully ignorant. There is no more demanding taskmaster in all the universe than the Lord. He demands our best twenty-four hours a day, and those who surrender themselves to full-time Christian service soon find this out.

Now, there are exceptions to this general rule laid down by Paul concerning the remuneration of those in Christian service. For example, Paul wrote to the church at Thessalonica in 1 Thessalonians 2:9, *"For ye remember, brethren, our labour and travail: for labouring night and day, because we would not be chargeable unto any of you, we preached unto you the gospel of God."* There were possibly two reasons why Paul worked during the day and preached at night at Thessalonica. One reason was that the membership was being accused by the rich Jews and idol-makers of every imaginable evil. So Paul did not want to bring an added accusation upon the church by the Jews who would have contended that he was only after their money. Also, the church at Thessalonica was a destitute church. The businessmen of the city had evidently taken economic measures against them, and they were probably not able to give Paul an honorarium, even if he would have accepted it. But the general rule remains, the servant of the Lord is worthy of his labors and within his rights to expect of the church funds to sustain himself and his family.

"Against an elder receive not an accusation,

but before two or three witnesses. Them that
sin rebuke before all, that others also may
fear. I charge thee before God, and the Lord
Jesus Christ, and the elect angels, that thou
observe these things without preferring one
before another, doing nothing by partiality"
(1 Tim. 5:19-21).

In these three verses Paul deals with calling those in positions of leadership to give an account for their stewardship before the congregation. If an elder, a pastor, a deacon, or a bishop commits an act that will bring shame upon their church and harm the testimony of the church before the world, that church leader is to be rebuked for this sin before the entire membership. This is to let both the membership and the world know that the church does not condone this man in his evil deed, and to bring the church leader who has sinned to open acknowledgement and repentence. If the sin is grievous enough, such a flagrant blasphemy, then other scriptures indicate that he can be deprived of his office and severed from the church rolls. But a charge is not to be brought before the congregation except by two or more witnesses. This is to prevent false malicious gossip from going too far. Paul makes it plain that gossip is not to be considered evidence — only facts as presented by two or more reliable witnesses. It is also evident that the public rebuke for Christian misconduct applies only to those in positions of leadership. The exhortation for the carnal and sinful habits of the membership is the duty of the pastor.

To bring accusations by individual members against other members, and to have everyone getting up in church and confessing their sins, would turn the general assembly into utter chaos and confusion. If you have some particular sin that is tempting you, consult with the pastor in private. But first of all, study the Scriptures to show yourself approved and judge yourself. We read in 1 Corinthians 11:31, *"For if we would judge ourselves, we should not be judged."* But even in judging ourselves, we should use spiritual discernment and not become overburdened with self-criticism. Often we receive letters where the writer displays a narrow view of his liberty in Christ. One will write that inasmuch as cleanliness is next to godliness, are they sinning if they wear their socks two days in succession? Another may want to know if they are guilty of the sin of gluttony if they put two pats of butter on their biscuit instead of one. Such petty personal matters do not fall into the category of sins that mar the testimony of the saints. The exhortation given by Paul concerning the rebuking of elders before the congregation is for the preservation of morally clean and spiritual leaders in the church, but today many pastors are giving sermons on the merits of adultery, the profit in fornication, the spiritual benefit of marijuana, and so on. The churches of today, for the most part, have not adhered to these admonitions given by Paul and this is why the church is not influencing the world.

We read in verse twenty-one that Paul charged Timothy and the church at Ephesus to be diligent in the matter "before God, the Lord Jesus Christ and the elect angels." The elect angels are those that remained faithful to God in contrast to the fallen angels, those angels mentioned by Jude who followed Satan and left their first estate. Paul's declaration here indicates that angels do have a part in the heavenly supervision of the church, and this strengthens our position that the seven angels to whom John wrote in Revelation 2 and 3 were actually angels and not human messengers of the churches. Reading next 1 Timothy 5:22:

> *"Lay hands suddenly on no man, neither be partaker of other men's sins: keep thyself pure."*

The reference to the laying on of hands is commonly interpreted to mean the ordination of deacons, elders, and pastors. Some interpret this to mean the welcoming of wayward church leaders back into the church. Either interpretation brings with it the same admonition. In other words, do not appoint Sunday school teachers, deacons, or pastors too quickly. When it comes to selecting men and women for full-time Christian service, words mean very little. We often find this out the hard way. Just because someone tells you what a dedicated Christian, talented, and dedicated worker they are, this doesn't mean that they necessarily are. We have learned to beware of those who puff themselves up and this is doubtless what Paul was referring to in 1 Timothy 5:22. Wait and let them prove themselves because when it comes to faithful Christian stewardship and dedication — actions speak louder than words. As far as reinstating wayward elders, deacons, and pastors, the admonition is to wait until they prove themselves, because if they have erred once, there is a good possibility they may err again. In this event, the church becomes partakers with them in their sins. Although Revelation 18:4 is to be understood literally, it can also be applied spiritually: ". . . *Come out of her, my people, that ye be not partakers of her sins, and that ye receive not of her plagues.*"

If leaders in your denomination utter blasphemous things against the Bible or the Lord Jesus Christ, then you become partakers with them in their blasphemy. If the money you contribute to your church is used for satanic causes, then you become accountable to God for the way your tithes and offerings are used.

> "*Drink no longer water, but use a little wine for thy stomach's sake and thine often infirmities*" (1 Tim. 5:23).

As we have mentioned before, it is thought by some that Timothy, though a faithful and dedicated Christian, was a shy and retiring sort of man and Paul had to prod him often to bring out his spiritual gifts and talents. Such a person is likely to have nervous problems that could manifest themselves in an ulcerated stomach. It is also possible that he may have had a gall bladder problem. In any event, there would have been no medicinal value in fermented wine. In fact, fermented wine would have been harmful to either ailment. Fruit juices are often recommended for certain ailments, especially gall bladder abnormalities. So it is my own opinion that Paul simply recommended that Timothy drink grape juice, and possibly other fruit juices, for his own body health, and we all could profit by this advice.

Reading next 1 Timothy 5:24-25:

> *"Some men's sins are open beforehand, going before to judgment; and some men they follow after. Likewise also the good works of some are manifest beforehand; and they that are otherwise cannot be hid."*

The last two verses are simply a summation of the entire chapter concerning wanton widows, those who do not care for their own, church leaders who bring shame and disgrace upon the testimony of the church by engaging in carnal sins before the world, and even those who become partakers with blasphemous church leaders in their sin. The conclusion of the whole matter is that no Christian gets away with anything. The Lord is observing us every day. Regardless of whether our failings and sins are going before us like a banner waving in the breeze, or following after us and hidden like a handkerchief in our back pocket, one day all our dirty linen will be put in the wash. We read in 1 Corinthians 3:13-15, *"Every man's work shall be made manifest: for the day shall declare it, because it shall be revealed by fire; and the fire shall try every man's work of what sort it is. If any man's work abide which he hath built thereupon, he shall receive a reward. If any man's work shall be burned, he shall suffer loss: but he himself shall be saved; yet so as by fire."*

This is why Paul closes the fifth chapter of his first epistle to Timothy by admonishing the Christians to do good works.

First Timothy, Chapter Six

"Let as many servants as are under the yoke count their own masters worthy of all honour, that the name of God and his doctrine be not blasphemed. And they that have believing masters, let them not despise them, because they are brethren; but rather do them service, because they are faithful and beloved, partakers of the benefit. These things teach and exhort. If any man teach otherwise, and consent not to wholesome words, even the words of our Lord Jesus Christ, and to the doctrine which is according to godliness; He is proud, knowing nothing, but doting about questions and strifes of words, whereof cometh envy, strife, railings, evil surmisings, Perverse disputings of men of corrupt minds, and destitute of the truth, supposing that gain is godliness: from such withdraw thyself" (1 Tim. 6:1-5).

Paul, having dealt with the economic obligations of the church to the needy and the correction of wayward Christian stewards, presents the correct position of the church toward the social and political issues of slavery. It is evident from Paul's exhortation on the subject that many were discontent with the church and felt that it should take a more active position in championing the freeing of the slaves, especially the freeing of slaves by Christian masters. The fact that slavery is the issue is brought forth emphatically by the reference to servants under the yoke. And regardless of the race of the slaves, the issue remained the same.

Slavery in the Roman Empire was an accepted fact. Almost every household in Rome, Greece, and many other provinces had slaves. Many of these slaves were bought in the slave markets as Rome extended its empire. It was not considered unethical or immoral in any way to have slaves. Many of the land owners who had slaves were saved by the gospel and added to the local church as members in good standing. Philemon, the master of Onesimus, was such a man. Some members of the church, and perhaps some outsiders, sought to establish the opposition to slavery as a basic church doctrine. But it was necessary for the leaders of the church to declare themselves on the issue. For example, Peter wrote in his first epistle: *"Servants, be subject to your masters with all fear; not only to the good and gentle, but also to the froward. For this is thankworthy, if a man for conscience toward God endure grief, suffering wrongfully. For what glory is it, if, when ye be buffeted for your faults, ye shall take it patiently? but if, when ye do well, and suffer for it, ye take it patiently, this is acceptable with*

God. For even hereunto were ye called: because Christ also suffered for us, leaving us an example, that ye should follow his steps" (1 Pet. 2:18-21).

There is no need for misunderstanding on this issue. The Scripture is plain and forthright as presented both by the apostle to the Jews, Peter, and the apostle to the Gentiles, Paul. Both agreed that Christian slaves were to pay honor to their masters, obey them, and even patiently bear cruel treatment without complaint. Even as Christ endured the scourging of the Romans, the Christian slaves were asked to show Christian restraint and love while they were likewise treated. It is evident from 1 Timothy 6:2 that slaves who belonged to Christian masters despised them because they would not relieve them of their bond. Both Paul and Peter said this should not be, because all believers belong to the family of God. On the other hand, Paul likewise entreated the Christian slave owners to deal kindly with their servants and look on Christian slaves as brothers. It would appear that Paul encouraged Onesimus to return to his master, but he reminded the Christian master in Philemon 1:15-16, *"For perhaps he therefore departed for a season, that thou shouldest receive him for ever; Not now as a servant, but above a servant, a brother beloved, specially to me, but how much more unto thee, both in the flesh, and in the Lord?"*

On the subject of slavery, Paul addressed himself only to Christian slaves and Christian masters, because he had no authority from the Lord to speak to non-

Christians on matters that related to a good Christian conscience. Many slaves were bonded to masters for an assortment of reasons — for livelihood, family debts, etc. Thus, Paul encouraged bond-servants, and even slaves, to fulfill their obligations to their masters. But to Christian masters he entreated them to accept their Christian servants as brothers in the Lord. To have openly opposed slavery would have brought the wrath of the Roman Empire upon the church and diminished the opportunity to win property owners and businessmen to the Lord.

The charge that the Christian faith condoned and even encouraged slavery is absolutely false. Nowhere in the New Testament does church doctrine either condone or encourage slavery. Through its appeal to Christians to manifest a good conscience toward God in all human relations, the Christian faith did more to abolish slavery than all the religions of the world put together.

What Paul, Peter, and other leaders of the Jewish and Gentile churches were opposed to was the use of the church to stir up revolutions against what some interpreted to be unjust social orders. This is not the purpose of the church. Paul said of men who would use the church in this fashion: *"He is proud, knowing nothing, but doting about questions and strifes of words, whereof cometh envy, strife, railings, evil surmisings, Perverse disputings of men of corrupt minds, and destitute of the truth, supposing that gain is godliness: from such withdraw thyself"* (1 Tim.

6:4-5). The gain spoken of here by Paul is social and political gain, as in the related subject — open opposition to slavery. All the modernists and social gospel leaders of the National Council of Churches and the World Council of Churches fall into the category of the men condemned so severely by Paul. They have advocated revolutions, and used money that has been contributed to the Lord's work to support them. Paul said, "from such withdraw thyself" (1 Tim. 6:5). This is a straightforward command to dissassociate yourself from churches and organizations that condone and support such abominable practices.

Paul moves on from the subject of slavery to the correct Christian attitude toward the material wealth of the world. While it is not closely related to slavery, Paul's admonition concerning making riches the goal of life is a rebuke against the rich Christians who kept slaves on their vast estates. We read in 1 Timothy 6:6-11:

> *"But godliness and contentment is great gain. For we brought nothing into this world, and it is certain we can carry nothing out. And having food and raiment let us be therewith content. But they that will be rich fall into temptation and a snare, and into many foolish and hurtful lusts, which drown men in destruction and perdition. For the love of money is the root of all evil: which while some coveted after, they have erred*

*from the faith, and pierced themselves
through with many sorrows. But thou, O
man of God, flee these things; and follow
after righteousness, godliness, faith, love,
patience, meekness."*

The central thought in the apostle's dissertation
on money is that the love of money is evil and will lead
the person to shipwreck his life because while loving
money, he will hate and despise everything else. The
most unhappy people in the world are those who
make the accumulation of a personal fortune their
goal in life. Paul warns Christians not to fall into this
snare of the devil.

In regard to the necessities of life, he encouraged
an attitude of godly contentment. Such an attitude
involves a recognition on the part of the believer that
God is the provider and we are to be thankful to Him
for that which we have. If Christians develop this
inward thankfulness, they are content with that which
they have. An example of the devil's snare entrapping
a man of God is the case of Solomon. Solomon
accumulated to himself a greater portion of the
world's wealth than any man before or after him. The
key words to Solomon's great downfall, as revealed in
Ecclesiastes, are "I," "me," or "mine." He said, *"I
communed with mine own heart . . . I am come to
great estate . . . I gave my heart to know wisdom . . ."*
(Eccl. 1:16-17). Solomon fell into the snare of the
devil, which is pride. It was pride that caused Lucifer's

downfall. Such a love of riches leads to great unhappiness, as we read in Ecclesiastes 2:17-18, *"Therefore I hated life; because the work that is wrought under the sun is grievous unto me: for all is vanity and vexation of spirit. Yea, I hated all my labour which I had taken under the sun: because I should leave it unto the man that shall be after me."* What bitterness and frustration it must be to a man who has worked all his life to build a great personal fortune, and then suddenly realize in his old age that he is going to have to leave it all behind for relatives to fight over.

The love of money, which means simply pride in material possessions, is the cruelist snare of the devil. If a Christian will consider everything that he has as belonging to the Lord, then such bitterness and disappointment with life will never overtake him. Thus, the great lesson which Paul would have all Christians learn is not to allow your own selfish pride to be built up in your own personal possessions. Paul emphasizes that *". . . righteousness, godliness, faith, love, patience,* [and] *meekness"* (1 Tim. 6:11), are of far greater value. Reading next 1 Timothy 6:12-13:

> *"Fight the good fight of faith, lay hold on eternal life, whereunto thou art also called, and hast professed a good profession before many witnesses. I give thee charge in the sight of God, who quickeneth all things, and before Christ Jesus, who before Pontius Pilate witnessed a good confession."*

Concerning Paul's reference to fighting the good fight of faith, I quote Dr. Kenneth Wuest:

"In the exhortation to Timothy, 'Fight the good fight of faith,' we have a reference to the Greek athletic games. Paul was educated so far as his Greek training was concerned, at the University of Tarsus, at that time the foremost Greek university in the world, outstripping the University of Athens, in its zeal for learning. The great apostle shows a first-hand acquaintance with Greek athletics in his writings, where he frequently uses them as illustrations of spiritual truth. Here he was writing to Timothy, whose father was a Greek. One of the chief activities of Roman life was the Greek games, held all over the empire. It was part of the atmosphere the Romans breathed. The verb 'fight' in the Greek means, 'to contend in the athletic games for the prize.' When we find that the gloves of the Greek boxer were fur-lined on the inside, but made on the outside of ox-hide with lead and iron sewed into it, and that the loser in a wrestling match had his eyes gouged out, we come to some apprecia-tion of what a Greek athletic contest consisted of. Thus, the word 'fight' had a very definite meaning for Timothy. Now, when Paul exhorts Timothy to lay hold of eternal life,

*he does not imply that he does not possess it.
Timothy was saved, and possessed eternal
life as a gift of God. What Paul was desirous
of was that Timothy experience more of
what this eternal life is in his life."*

Paul again referred to the good fight in his second
epistle to Timothy: *"For I am now ready to be offered,
and the time of my departure is at hand. I have fought
a good fight, I have finished my course, I have kept the
faith: Henceforth there is laid up for me a crown of
righteousness, which the Lord, the righteous judge,
shall give me at that day: and not to me only, but unto
all them also that love his appearing"* (2 Tim. 4:6-8).

These words to Timothy were written just before
Paul's execution at the hands of the Roman government. The meaning here is that in the warfare that
involves the Christian and the world, the flesh and the
devil, Paul had indeed fought a good fight, all the way
to the end of the contest. However, the world,
representing the Roman government, had a sword at
Paul's throat. In the arenas of Rome, the winner in
good standing would be given a crown, often weaved
from roses or olive branches. The fate of the fallen
gladiator was submitted to the favor of the crowd. If
the audience held their thumbs up, his life would be
spared. If the audience turned their thumbs down, he
would be beheaded. So Paul meant here that the
world had turned their thumbs down on him and he
would soon be taken out and beheaded. And though

he would receive no crown from this world, the Lord Jesus Christ was waiting to bestow upon his head the greatest crown of all, the crown of righteousness. And so it is with all Christians — expect no crowns from this present world. Fight a good fight of faith and the greatest judge of all, the Lord Jesus Christ, will personally place the victory crown upon your brow. Let us read 1 Timothy 6:13 again, *"I give thee charge in the sight of God, who quickeneth all things, and before Christ Jesus, who before Pontius Pilate witnessed a good confession."*

The confession of Jesus and the acknowledgement of Pilate is recorded in John 18:35-40; 19:1-5: *"Pilate answered, Am I a Jew? Thine own nation and the chief priests have delivered thee unto me: what hast thou done? Jesus answered, My kingdom is not of this world: if my kingdom were of this world, then would my servants fight, that I should not be delivered to the Jews: but now is my kingdom not from hence. Pilate therefore said unto him, Art thou a king then? Jesus answered, Thou sayest that I am a king. To this end was I born, and for this cause came I into the world, that I should bear witness unto the truth. Every one that is of the truth heareth my voice. Pilate saith unto him, What is truth? And when he had said this, he went out again unto the Jews, and saith unto them, I find in him no fault at all. But ye have a custom, that I should release unto you one at the passover: will ye therefore that I release unto you the King of the Jews? Then cried they all again, saying, Not this man, but*

Barabbas. Now Barabbas was a robber. Then Pilate therefore took Jesus, and scourged him. And the soldiers platted a crown of thorns, and put it on his head, and they put on him a purple robe, And said, Hail, King of the Jews! and they smote him with their hands. Pilate therefore went forth again, and saith unto them, Behold, I bring him forth to you, that ye may know that I find no fault in him. Then came Jesus forth, wearing the crown of thorns, and the purple robe. And Pilate saith unto them, Behold the man!"

The stand which Jesus Christ took before His judge of this world, Pilate, signified the stand which Christians should take before the world. Our kingdom is not of this world because we are citizens of Heaven, destined to reign and rule with our eternal King, the Lord Jesus Christ. We are here on earth to bear witness to the truth that Jesus Christ died for the sins of the world and He is coming back as King of kings and Lord of lords.

Jesus Christ refuted any political ambitions upon the province of Judah or the Roman Empire. Nevertheless, he did not advocate His right to be king of Israel, because in the age to come, He will reign on David's throne. He answered every question truthfully. As the true Word of God, He could not have done otherwise. When the interrogation ended, his political judge, Pilate, said, "I find no fault in this man." And this is the admonition which Paul wrote to Timothy, and it applies to each one of us who names the name of Christ.

*"That thou keepest this commandment
without spot, unrebukeable, until the appearing of our Lord Jesus Christ: Which in his
times he shall shew, who is the blessed and
only Potentate, the King of kings, and Lord
of lords; Who only hath immortality, dwelling
in the light which no man can approach
unto; whom no man hath seen, nor can see:
to whom be honour and power everlasting.
Amen"* (1 Tim. 6:14-16).

These verses are directly related to the confession
of Christ before Pilate. The exhortations and instructions given by Paul to Timothy are extended to all
churches for doctrine and obedience in the faith from
that time until the second coming of Christ. Paul
called "the appearing" or revealing of Jesus Christ as
the sovereign ruler of the universe, the King over all
who are kings, and Lord over all who are called lords.
This will occur, according to Paul, "in his time"
referred to in other places of the New Testament as the
"day of Christ." The world had its day when Pilate
turned Christ over to the mob for crucifixion, but the
Lord will have His day when He returns to put the
world under His absolute authority. This glorious
scene is described in Revelation 19:11-16: *"And I saw
heaven opened, and behold a white horse; and he that
sat upon him was called Faithful and True, and in
righteousness he doth judge and make war. His eyes
were as a flame of fire, and on his head were many*

crowns; and he had a name written, that no man knew, but he himself. And he was clothed with a vesture dipped in blood: and his name is called The Word of God. And the armies which were in heaven followed him upon white horses, clothed in fine linen, white and clean. And out of his mouth goeth a sharp sword, that with it he should smite the nations: and he shall rule them with a rod of iron: and he treadeth the winepress of the fierceness and wrath of Almighty God. And he hath on his vesture and on his thigh a name written, KING OF KINGS, AND LORD OF LORDS."

This is the blessed hope and Paul admonished all Christians to confess this glorious truth before the world — the Lord Jesus Christ is coming back to save the world from those who would destroy it. We continue in our study and read 1 Timothy 6:17-19:

> *"Charge them that are rich in this world, that they be not highminded, nor trust in uncertain riches, but in the living God, who giveth us richly all things to enjoy; That they do good, that they be rich in good works, ready to distribute, willing to communicate; Laying up in store for themselves a good foundation against the time to come, that they may lay hold on eternal life."*

In these three verses Paul has a final word to say to Timothy concerning the wealthy members of the congregation — those who are rich in the goods of this world. They are to be reminded that there is nothing more uncertain than wealth. A man can be wealthy one day and poor the next; therefore, let those with riches be ready to share their wealth with the church and those who are in need. This is not a church-sponsored charity program which Paul had in mind here, but rather a Christian obligation on the part of the individual believer. The rich members had a habit of forming together in their own little social clique, so Paul reminds them to communicate with others, and especially the unsaved. Paul communicated the gospel to every nation he visited. He was always on the go communicating the good news that Christ died for the sins of the world. The growth of Christianity is based on communications. This is why we are on the air — communicating the gospel. But even so, the responsibility of gospel communications extends to every Christian. Unless you communicate the message of salvation and what being a Christian means to your heart to loved ones and neighbors, you are failing in your responsibility. One of the faults of the rich members of the church at Ephesus was that they did not communicate the Christian message, and this remains one of the principal failings of many rich church members even today. In verse nineteen, Paul again reminds the Christians of the importance of laying up in heavenly store a good foundation. This good foundation has reference to good works which are built upon our faith in Jesus Christ whereby we were saved. *"For other foundation can no man lay than that is laid, which is Jesus Christ. Now if any man build upon this foundation gold, silver, precious stones, wood, hay, stubble . . . If any man's work abide which he hath built thereupon, he shall receive a reward. If any man's work shall be burned, he shall suffer loss: but he himself shall be saved; yet so as by fire"* (1 Cor. 3:11-12, 14-15).

So Paul reminds Christians that riches on earth have no relation to our riches in Heaven. We continue by reading the last two verses of Paul's first epistle to Timothy:

> *"O Timothy, keep that which is committed to thy trust, avoiding profane and vain babblings, and oppositions of science falsely so called: Which some professing have erred concerning the faith. Grace be with thee. Amen"* (1 Tim. 6:20-21).

The final admonition given in this pastoral epistle to the Christian church is to beware of the oppositions of pseudo-science. This warning applies more to our day than it ever has in the past. Science, so-called, has taken over the teaching of our children in the schools. The children are taught that science has found the answer to life in the theory of evolution. The children are informed that the scientists, not the Bible, hold the truth to man's past and present. Everyone is encouraged to look upon science as the great inventor of truth. But science has never invented a single truth. Science has only been able to uncover a small portion of the truth, and this is like taking one piece of a puzzle and constructing the entire picture from ninety-nine percent imagination. Science did not invent the atom; it only discovered it.

The Associated Press once reported on interviews they had conducted with several of the highest church officials in the major denominations. They were all asked the relationship of faith to science in the space age, and these modernists all stammered and stuttered, but the consensus was that modern man was finding it difficult to believe in God, and eventually science would negate the need for faith and men would soon be walking completely by sight. What all this means is that soon there will be no church according to these modernists.

But the big question today is: If science holds the answer to life, why are there so many people searching for meaning and purpose in life? Millions are wandering off into the occult, the drug culture, alcoholism, and suicide.

In the November 1970 edition of the *Bible-Science Newsletter*, there is this remarkable parable which exposes the folly of looking upon science as the paragon of truth:

> *"This is the title of a paper by Professor Gary Park of Eastern Baptist College in Muncie, Indiana. He begins with a para-*

trooper who lands on a small island in the Pacific, but in landing his parachute was snagged in a tree and he fell to the ground unconscious and later suffered from amnesia. From logic he attempts to reconstruct who he is, where he came from, and what he is doing there. He concludes that he must be some sort of cousin to the apes on the island. He sees his parachute dangling from the tree with a pile of broken wood under it. His logical conclusion was that he had got there by sea, and he had the facts to prove it — broken wood, the remnants of the raft he had used, and the parachute which had been the sail. Rationally, he could not reach the conclusion that he had arrived by air, for a rationalist cannot go beyond his experience or understanding. In his state of amnesia, he did not remember that airplanes existed and nothing in his experience on the island suggested that airplanes could exist. In fact, he could 'prove' that flight is impossible. Some might argue that eventually he would have discovered that flight is possible. This is a practical notion in science, but not in philosophy. . . . Going back to our paratrooper — eventually he discovers something which had been hidden by the parachute. It was a small black book in which he read his name, that he was a member of the NASA space team who had been dropped from the air, onto a small, uncharted island in the Pacific Ocean, that his mission was one of survival and to improve the island, and that he would be picked up before the stormy season. In our lives, this book is the Bible, and it tells us about our origin, our purpose in life, and our destiny. The paratrooper had to make a choice — could he believe the book or was it just a myth? Didn't science and logic tell him he came by sea? He finally had to make a choice between faith and his own limited experience or faith in a power beyond himself, and we must make the same choice."

The question facing the paratrooper was: Should he trust his own scientific conclusions and try to save himself? Or, should he believe what was written in the book and wait for his deliverance? Likewise, a similar question faces each of us. Do you by faith believe what the Bible says in John 3:16? Or, do you follow the reasoning of science as it blindly feels its way along attempting to uncover truth? If the paratrooper followed his own reasoning, he was doubtless lost; if he accepted what was written in the book, he was saved.

The issue between God and the world today is whether to have faith in the inspired Word, or to believe scientific atheism. Paul knew that of all the wiles of the devil, this would be a great issue as the world was being prepared for the coming of Christ.

Part Two

Second Timothy

Chapter One

We begin our study of the last epistle of Paul by reading 2 Timothy 1:1-2:

> *"Paul, an apostle of Jesus Christ by the will of God, according to the promise of life which is in Christ Jesus, To Timothy, my dearly beloved son: Grace, mercy, and peace, from God the Father and Christ Jesus our Lord."*

In the salutation, Paul identifies himself as the writer of the letter and Timothy as the person to whom it is addressed. Paul also refers to himself as that "Paul" who is "an apostle of Jesus Christ." An apostle is one who is appointed to act, or represent another person. An apostle is appointed to duty because it is not convenient, or possible, for the sender to go himself. However, an apostle is to act in the place of the sender just as if the sender were there himself. In other words, Paul was to represent Jesus Christ to the Gentiles just as if Jesus were there Himself. We read in Ephesians 3:1-2, *"For this cause I Paul, the prisoner of Jesus Christ for you Gentiles, If ye have heard of the dispensation of the grace of God which is given me to you-ward."*

Paul was sent specifically to the Gentiles by Jesus Christ. Many, including some at the Jerusalem congregation, continually questioned Paul's right to be called an apostle, because they contended that he was not personally chosen by Jesus Christ. However, Paul steadfastly maintained that he personally had seen Jesus on the road to Damascus, and it was at that time that the Lord appointed Paul to be a special apostle. This all came about in accordance with the will of God, meaning that God had planned for this man, Saul of Tarsus, to be saved that he might declare the promise of life through faith in Jesus Christ, the only begotten Son of God, to the Gentile world.

In verse two, Paul refers to Timothy as "my dearly beloved son." In 1 Timothy 1:2, Timothy is called "my own son in the faith." It is probable that Paul led Timothy to an acceptance of Jesus Christ as Savior and Lord when the apostle visited the home of Timothy's mother at Derbe (Acts 16:1-3). In any event, Timothy was very dear to Paul. Although quite young, Paul appointed him as bishop over the churches of Asia Minor, and Timothy is the only person in all the Bible to have two books specifically addressed to him.

In concluding the salutation, Paul extends to Timothy his prayer for *"Grace, mercy, and peace, from God our Father and Jesus Christ our Lord."* We continually need God's grace and mercy. We are saved by grace, and we are kept by grace — nothing depends upon us.

> *"I thank God, whom I serve from my forefathers with pure conscience, that without ceasing I have remembrance of thee in my prayers night and day; Greatly desiring to see thee, being mindful of thy tears, that I may be filled with joy; When I call to remembrance the unfeigned faith that is in thee, which dwelt first in thy grandmother Lois, and thy mother Eunice; and I am persuaded that in thee also"* (2 Tim. 1:3-5).

In his opening remarks, Paul declares that he served God with a pure conscience. The word "conscience" is not found in the Old Testament. Before the flood, God instituted human government to restrain the wickedness of men. Then came the law through Moses to show men and women that which was right and wrong in God's sight. The role of the conscience in the lives of men and women was initiated, or at least enlarged, with the coming of Jesus Christ and the Holy Spirit into the world.

Conscience is an instinctive knowledge as to the right or wrong of our moral, or immoral deeds. Conscience is the property of, or at least influenced by, the Holy Spirit, in both the saved and unsaved. Jesus said: *"Nevertheless I tell you the truth; It is expedient for you that I go away: for if I go not away, the Comforter will not come unto you; but if I depart,*

I will send him unto you. And when he is come, he will reprove the world of sin, and of righteousness, and of judgment: Of sin, because they believe not on me; Of righteousness, because I go to my Father, and ye see me no more; Of judgment, because the prince of this world is judged" (John 16:7-11).

In the New Testament, we find several types of conscience:

- *A convicting conscience* — a conscience that convicts the sinner of sin (John 8:9).
- *A seared conscience* — where the individual so resists his conscience concerning evil that it becomes like scar tissue left by a burn, insensitive (1 Tim. 4:2).
- *A purged conscience* — The conscience of a guilty man that has been purged by the blood of Jesus Christ, convincing him that his sins have been forgiven (Heb. 9:14).
- *A pure conscience* — the conscience of those in God's service where nothing is hidden from God or man (1 Tim. 3:8-9; 2 Tim. 1:3).
- *A weak conscience* — the conscience of a carnal Christian who has not matured in the faith, like the weak Christians at Corinth (1 Cor. 8:7).
- *A defiled conscience* — the conscience of a person who claims to be a Christian while knowingly and willingly doing evil (Tit. 1:15-16).
- *A satisfied conscience* — a good conscience that refuses to be intimidated by self-righteous and

judging church members (1 Cor. 10:25-29).

Therefore, Paul declared to Timothy that he had a good conscience toward God in that he had fulfilled his mission to preach the gospel to the Gentiles and also to bear witness of Jesus Christ to his own people, Israel. It is when Christians take communion that God commands us to search our own conscience. Paul declared that he possessed a pure conscience, not for the purpose of boasting, but to encourage Timothy to likewise keep a good conscience toward both God and man.

It is difficult for us to understand the conditions in which Paul was confined when he wrote his last epistle. While on tour, we visited the prison where the apostle and other Christians of that day were confined prior to execution. There is no comparison between that prison and the prisons of today. The cells themselves are nothing more than tiny stone cages with a small barred window at the front. Yet in these depressing and filthy circumstances, Paul remembered to pray for Timothy in his responsibilities over the church at Ephesus.

The reference to tears that Timothy must have shed at their last parting indicated once again the close father-son relationship that existed between the two. In verse five of the first chapter, the reference made to the great faith of Timothy's grandmother Lois, and his mother Eunice is a combination of Christian courtesy and a reaffirmation of the affection between

Timothy's loved ones and the apostle. Nothing is said
of Timothy's father. He was a Greek and probably an
idol worshipper. The omission of his name indicates
that Timothy and his father had little in common and
probably were never very close.

The biographical sketch of Timothy provided for
us in the Scriptures is as follows:

- In Acts 16:1-2, Timothy is described as a disciple of
  Jesus Christ who had a good reputation among the
  brethren. This was in the year A.D. 52 and he was
  probably no more than twenty years of age.
- Timothy was with Paul when he wrote his epistle to
  the Romans in A.D. 57 (Rom. 16:21).
- Paul trusted Timothy to visit the church at Corinth
  and strengthen them in the faith. This was also in
  the year A.D. 57. While Timothy was evidently a
  sensitive and sincere young man, he was not as
  eloquent in speech or impressive in appearance as
  Apollos. Therefore, Paul entreated the elders of the
  church at Corinth to receive Timothy warmly and
  with confidence in order that he not be ill at ease or
  fearful (1 Cor. 16:10).
- In the year A.D. 58, Timothy was with Paul at
  Philippi when he wrote the second epistle to the
  Corinthians. Paul commended Timothy for effec-
  tively preaching Jesus Christ when he went to
  Corinth (2 Cor. 1:1; 2 Cor. 1:19).
- In the year A.D. 63, Timothy was with Paul in Rome.
  While Paul was in prison, it would appear that

Timothy was still free. And while most of Paul's fellow workers had deserted him, Timothy faithfully remained with him, ministering to his needs. The faithfulness of Timothy and his devotion is declared by the apostle: *"But I trust in the Lord Jesus to send Timotheus shortly unto you, that I also may be of good comfort, when I know your state. For I have no man likeminded, who will naturally care for your state. For all seek their own, not the things which are Jesus Christ's. But ye know the proof of him, that, as a son with the father, he hath served with me in the gospel. Him therefore I hope to send presently, so soon as I shall see how it will go with me. But I trust in the Lord that I also myself shall come shortly"* (Phil. 2:19-24). The other men who traveled with Paul departed to their wives, homes, and businesses; only Timothy remained. It would seem that Timothy was not married, and in all things put the affairs of God over the affairs of the world. However, his unmarried status may have been a problem to him (2 Tim. 2:22), and it is probable that he took a wife later in life.

- Timothy was released from prison, probably in late A.D. 64, and as indicated by Paul in Hebrews 13:23-24, they traveled together to revisit the churches, and may have even gone to Jerusalem.

- Luke and Timothy were Paul's most valued co-workers; however, Timothy was the closer of the two to the apostle, and he was used to confirm the churches in faith and doctrine (1 Thess. 3:2).

We continue by reading 2 Timothy 1:6:
*"Wherefore I put thee in remembrance that
thou stir up the gift of God, which is in thee
by the putting on of my hands."*

It could be misconstrued that Timothy had
become apathetic in conducting church business and
his own personal ministry, but this is not necessarily
so. Paul thought of Timothy like his own son, and like
a father, he gave the young man plenty of advice. For
example, we read in 1 Timothy 4:11-14, *"These things
command and teach. Let no man despise thy youth;
but be thou an example of the believers, in word, in
conversation, in charity, in spirit, in faith, in purity.
Till I come, give attendance to reading, to exhortation,
to doctrine. Neglect not the gift that is in thee, which
was given thee by prophecy, with the laying on of the
hands of the presbytery."*

The word for stir up in the Greek means "to
rekindle."So Paul reminded Timothy in both of his
letters to him to remain on fire for God. The same
admonition could apply to all of us, and especially to
us in full-time Christian service. It is easy to fall into a
rut where we let duties and responsibilities so
overwhelm us until we lose sight of our real mission —
to preach the gospel for the saving of souls, and
declare the blessed hope in these last days.

*"For God hath not given us the spirit of fear;
but of power, and of love, and of a sound*

mind. Be not thou therefore ashamed of the testimony of our Lord, nor of me his prisoner: but be thou partaker of the afflictions of the gospel according to the power of God; Who hath saved us, and called us with an holy calling, not according to our works, but according to his own purpose and grace, which was given us in Christ Jesus before the world began, But is now made manifest by the appearing of our Saviour Jesus Christ, who hath abolished death, and hath brought life and immortality to light through the gospel: Whereunto I am appointed a preacher, and an apostle, and a teacher of the Gentiles" (2 Tim. 1:7-11).

In the year A.D. 67 Christians were under extreme persecution. Nero was the Roman Ceasar at the time, and believers were imprisoned, forced to fight the gladiators in the theater, fed to the lions to the delight of spectators, or burned at the stake after being coated with tar. The more socially or politically prominent, like Paul, were imprisoned and disgraced. Also, to befriend or associate with Christians in prison brought economic, political, and social reprisals. Paul brings out in this letter to Timothy that many were ashamed of him and even longtime friends and fellow workers in the gospel deserted him out of shame or fear. Also, because prison conditions were so terrible, many went insane after an extended period of confinement.

Therefore, the apostle, in his extreme loneliness and grief over being forsaken, reminds Timothy that God does not give a spirit of fear. In times of imprisonment and sufferings, God becomes a comforter and sustainer. There are numerous accounts of American prisoners of war during World War II, the Korean War, and the Vietnam War, who were victorious over their captors because they were Christians. They relied on the power of God to mentally lift themselves above their circumstances, and to love and pray for their tormentors and jailors. So Paul assures Timothy that he was not fearful, but of sound mind and strong in the faith.

There are three principal things that Paul said God gives to every Christian:

1. *Power* — The word Paul used for power in the Greek was *dunamis*, from which we get our word "dynamo." In Ephesians 3:20 Paul refers to the presence of Jesus Christ in our hearts as a "power that worketh in us." So the power of God in Christians is like a working dynamo. While a dynamo is idle, or just sitting there, nothing happens. But once it begins to turn, a powerful current streams from it. Just so, the power of God is in every Christian, but like the dynamo, it has to be turned on — exercised by faith. Through the exercise of this power of God, Paul became a mighty evangelist and the apostle to the Gentiles. It was by this power that he wrote over one-half of the

books of the New Testament, faced lions, overcame repeated beatings, and refused to let prison and chains break his spirit. He wrote to the brethren in one of his prison epistles, *". . . I was made a minister, according to the gift of the grace of God given unto me by the effectual working of his power"* (Eph. 3:7). So the most important item that God equips every Christian with is power.

2. *Spirit of Love* — God gives every Christian the spirit of love. I realize that it appears to be either dormant or dead in most believers today; nevertheless, God's love is imparted to every Christian. The ability to love others, even our enemies and tormentors, is one of the greatest assets a Christian owns. In all his prison epistles, Paul never said one word against his captors. Rather, he gloried in his sufferings and tribulations because in them he became identified with Jesus Christ in His like troubles. The word used for love in 2 Timothy 1:7 is *agape*, which does not mean a human love or emotion, but rather a "divine love." It is a love beyond human feeling or understanding. Paul said of this kind of love in Romans 5:3-5, *". . . we glory in tribulations also: knowing that tribulation worketh patience; And patience, experience; and experience, hope: And hope maketh not ashamed; because the love of God is shed abroad in our hearts by the Holy Ghost which is given unto us."* In order for God's love in us to bring joy to Christians and be effective in reaching others for the Lord, it must be

shared, or shed abroad. I have been to Israel many times, and yet I never cease to marvel at the difference between the Sea of Galilee and the Dead Sea. Although just a few miles apart, and both fed by the same stream, they are completely opposite in appearance. The Sea of Galilee is clear, has beautiful foliage on the shoreline, and is alive with all kinds of fish and birds. The Dead Sea on the other hand is stagnant and inactive, has little or no foliage along the shoreline, and any fish that enter from the Jordan River immediately die. The reason for the difference in the two bodies of water is that the Sea of Galilee allows the water it receives to flow through it, while the Dead Sea keeps all that it gets. The only way any water escapes from the Dead Sea is through evaporation, and even then, all of the salts, fertilizers, and minerals are retained. Likewise, Christians usually fall into two categories — Sea of Galilee Christians or Dead Sea Christians. What makes the difference is shedding the love of God abroad to others. *Agape* is translated "charity" in 1 Corinthians: *"Though I speak with the tongues of men and of angels, and have not charity, I am become as sounding brass, or a tinkling cymbal. And though I have the gift of prophecy, and understand all mysteries, and all knowledge; and though I have all faith, so that I could remove mountains, and have not charity, I am nothing"* (1 Cor. 13:1-2).

3. *Sound Mind* — The third thing that God gives to

every Christian is a sound mind. This means that Christians can have a mind that will not be shaken by the things of this world, regardless of how unpleasant they are — divorce, death, sickness, imprisonment, sorrow, heartaches, or any tribulation. Certainly, we will feel sadness and disappointment, and even may hurt and suffer for an extended period of time. Nevertheless, just as Jesus overcame all sorrow and sufferings, Christians can likewise emerge victorious, because God has given us a like mind that will triumph. But just as the power of God must be exercised like a dynamo, and the love of God must be shed abroad, the mind of Christ in the Christian must be renewed. In other words, the things of the world must be repulsed and expunged, and the things of God be introduced and cherished. This is a day-by-day process. We read in 1 Corinthians 2:16, ". . . *we have the mind of Christ.*" And again in Romans 12:2, ". . . *be not conformed to this world: but be ye transformed by the renewing of your mind, that ye may prove what is that good, and acceptable, and perfect, will of God.*"

Now, for the reason that God has given the Christian the spirit of power, the spirit of love, and of a sound mind, Paul exhorts Timothy to be faithful in observing three commandments:

1. *Do not be ashamed of the gospel, which is the testimony of Jesus Christ.* Regardless of how

politically or socially embarrassing, or dangerous it may become to witness and preach the gospel, Christians are not to be ashamed. A parallel today to the conditions that Paul and Timothy faced would be Russia, where Christians are second-rate citizens. Many have been killed and imprisoned in the last fifty years.

2. *Do not be ashamed to be a friend, or a co-laborer with those who preach the gospel.* Many of Paul's former friends had grown ashamed of his imprisonment. They became reticent to admit that they were an associate of a man charged with criminal acts by the Roman government. It is not that Paul doubted Timothy's faithfulness and friendship; however, when all others were forsaking him, the apostle needed assurance from Timothy's own lips, or words in writing, that he was still standing with him.

3. *Do not shun afflictions if such persecutions result from declaring the gospel.* The two ministers of God were living in an age when to openly preach the gospel often meant persecution, and even death. So Paul encouraged Timothy to continue to preach the Word and not allow fear or threat of afflictions to silence him as it had done to others. Paul testified of his own afflictions for the preaching of the gospel: *". . . I am more; in labours more abundant, in stripes above measure, in prisons more frequent, in deaths oft. Of the Jews five times received I forty stripes save one. Thrice was I beaten with rods, once*

*was I stoned, thrice I suffered shipwreck, a night
and a day I have been in the deep; In journeyings
often, in perils of waters, in perils of robbers, in
perils by mine own countrymen, in perils by the
heathen, in perils in the city, in perils in the
wilderness, in perils in the sea, in perils among false
brethren; In weariness and painfulness, in watchings
often, in hunger and thirst, in fastings often, in cold
and nakedness. Beside those things that are without,
that which cometh upon me daily, the care of all the
churches"* (2 Cor. 11:23-28).

In 2 Timothy 1:9-11, Paul enumerates the eight-fold works of God concerning the Christian from beginning to eternity:

1. God saved us through the power of the gospel.
2. He called us with a holy calling.
3. We were saved and chosen to fulfill God's purpose;
   therefore, our salvation and calling was according
   to grace, and not in recognition of anything we had
   done or earned.
4. God's plan for the eternal future of Christians in
   His kingdom was formulated before the world was
   created.
5. This plan was made manifest, or revealed in all its
   glory, when Jesus Christ appeared on earth as Lord
   and Savior.
6. Jesus Christ abolished the hold that death has over
   all who are saved.

7. Jesus Christ brought the gift of God, eternal life for the soul and immortality for the body, to light, or made this truth open to all men, through the preaching of the gospel.

8. The Apostle Paul was appointed a preacher and teacher to the Gentiles to declare this gospel.

We continue in our study by reading 2 Timothy 1:12:

> *"For the which cause I also suffer these things: nevertheless I am not ashamed: for I know whom I have believed, and am persuaded that he is able to keep that which I have committed unto him against that day."*

Paul concludes, for Timothy's benefit and admonition, that seeing how God has so carefully and completely planned our future for us and given us the assurance of these eternal gifts, he is content to suffer all things for this great purpose. He continues to say that he is not ashamed before men, because he knows the One whom he represents as His apostle. Paul is also assured that his own labors in the gospel which have been committed, or deposited with the Lord, will be kept in trust until that day, meaning the Judgment Seat of Christ when Christians will receive a reward for works they have done here in the flesh.

In the next two verses, Paul commands Timothy to cherish and guard that which has been put under his authority — the preaching of the gospel:

"Hold fast the form of sound words, which thou hast heard of me, in faith and love which is in Christ Jesus. That good thing which was committed unto thee keep by the Holy Ghost which dwelleth in us" (2 Tim. 1:13-14).

Paul gives two charges to the young bishop of Ephesus:

1. *Hold fast, or securely, the outline or substance of the gospel passed on to Timothy by Paul.* The meaning is that this is a message that came from Jesus Christ to save whosoever would believe. It must not be changed or altered in any way. He must continue to tell men and women everywhere how to be saved, just as he was saved.
2. *He was also to keep guard over the gospel.* Although Timothy himself would be faithful to the leading of the Holy Spirit in interpreting the gospel and preaching it to men, others might not. Therefore, as a church leader of considerable authority, he was to jealously guard that gospel which Paul had given him to preach, not letting others in the churches under his care either distort or subvert it.

Thus, in his second epistle to Timothy, Paul impresses upon us the sacred trust that God has committed to all of us who believe and are saved by the gospel. It is a great plan, a perfect plan, an eternal plan, whereby we receive eternal life through faith in that which Jesus Christ did for us on the cross. He took our place, abolished the hold that death has over us, and brought us all into the light of life and immortality.

We continue and read 2 Timothy 1:15:

> *"This thou knowest, that all they which are in Asia be turned away from me; of whom are Phygellus and Hermogenes."*

There are some commentaries which espouse the view that Paul was referring only to the church members from Asia who were visiting in Rome. However, we agree with the position taken by Dr. Kenneth Wuest, and we quote his remarks:

> *"Asia is not here to be understood as the continent of that name, but preconsular Asia, which included Mysia, Lydia, Caria, a great part of Phrygia, the Troad, and the islands off the coast. This would include the western part of what we used to know as Asia Minor, but which today is called Turkey. It comprises the provinces bordering the Aegean Sea, except Phrygia, which is inland. Paul says that all the believers in this territory had turned away from him. But this*

> *turning away was not for mere personal*
> *reasons, as the context indicates. In 1:13, 14,*
> *the apostle had just been speaking of the*
> *necessity for guarding and defending the*
> *truth, and in 2:17, 18, the two individuals*
> *mentioned in verse 15, are said to be involved*
> *in a departure from true doctrine. It was for*
> *doctrinal reasons that those in Asia turned*
> *away from Paul."*

Even before Paul was imprisoned, the church in Galatia had departed from the doctrine of Jesus Christ as set forth by the apostle. He wrote in Galatians 1:6, *"I marvel that ye are so soon removed from him that called you into the grace of Christ unto another gospel."*

When Paul revisited Asia, he evidently discovered that most of the believers there had followed those in Galatia. This departure from the faith was later revealed by the Apostle John in the message to the seven churches of Asia in the Book of Revelation.

> *"The Lord give mercy unto the house of*
> *Onesiphorus; for he oft refreshed me, and*
> *was not ashamed of my chain: But, when he*
> *was in Rome, he sought me out very*
> *diligently, and found me. The Lord grant*
> *unto him that he may find mercy of the Lord*
> *in that day: and in how many things he*
> *ministered unto me at Ephesus, thou knowest*

very well" (2 Tim. 1:16-18).

Onesiphorus was evidently a member of the church at Ephesus, and Paul wanted Timothy to know how diligently, at great risk, this man had ministered to his needs in Rome. Onesiphorus came to see Paul often while he was in Rome, doubtless bringing him food, clothing, and whatever would make Paul's burden lighter. From the context regarding Paul's commendation of Onesiphorus, we know he had died. It is entirely possible that he suffered martyrdom. This is revealed in Paul's statement, "The Lord give mercy unto the house of Onesiphorus." Nothing is said about greeting Onesiphorus himself. Paul's prayer was that the love and care that this faithful Christian had extended to him in time of great need would be taken into account by the Lord when rewards are given at the Judgment Seat of Christ.

Chapter Two

"Thou therefore, my son, be strong in the grace that is in Christ Jesus. And the things that thou hast heard of me among many witnesses, the same commit thou to faithful men, who shall be able to teach others also. Thou therefore endure hardness, as a good soldier of Jesus Christ" (2 Tim. 2:1-3).

Paul had learned many lessons through experience, and one of these lessons was that a minister cannot compromise the gospel of Christ. Any sign of compromise is an indication of weakness. While Paul was all things to all men that he might win them with the gospel, he was unwavering when it came to matters of doctrine. We may well wonder just why Paul would exhort Timothy to "be strong in the grace that is in Christ Jesus" and to "endure hardness as a good soldier." Perhaps Timothy was not as bold as Paul, or more refined in the social sense; therefore, he needed to be encouraged to speak out forcefully and stand up against those who would pervert the gospel. Those who have had marine or infantry training are eventually conditioned to make survival a matter of going on rather than giving up.

Christians are to think of themselves as soldiers in the war that is raging between God and the devil. This war began when Satan, in his pride, decided to raise his throne above the stars of God (Isa. 14:12-17). This is the motivation behind Paul's admonition to the church at Ephesus in Ephesians 6:10-11, *"Finally, my brethren, be strong in the Lord, and in the power of his might. Put on the whole armour of God, that ye may be able to stand against the wiles of the devil."* The same language was used by Paul in his first letter to Timothy. *"This charge I commit unto thee, son Timothy, according to the prophecies which went before on thee, that thou by them mightest war a good warfare'* (1 Tim. 1:18).

The spiritual warfare between the forces of God and Satan is also indicated in the tenth chapter of Daniel, and a forthcoming battle of supreme importance is prophesied in Revelation 12:7-8: *"And there was war in heaven: Michael and his angels fought against the dragon; and the dragon fought and his angels, And prevailed not; neither was their place found any more in heaven."* As Christians, we are a part of this continuing war. Our battle arena is here on earth — fighting the good fight of faith for the souls of men.

Timothy was also exhorted once again to commit those things which Paul had committed to him before the presbytery to men of like faith. This committment is recorded in 1 Timothy 6:12-14, 17, 20: *"Fight the good fight of faith, lay hold on eternal life, whereunto thou art also called, and hast professed a good profession before many witnesses. I give thee charge in the sight of God, who quickeneth all things, and before Christ Jesus, who before Pontius Pilate witnessed a good confession; That thou keep this commandment without spot, unrebukeable, until the appearing of our Lord Jesus Christ . . . Charge them that are rich in this world, that they be not highminded, nor trust in uncertain riches, but in the living God, who giveth us richly all things to enjoy . . . O Timothy, keep that which is committed to thy trust, avoiding profane and vain babblings, oppositions of science falsely so called."*

We continue with 2 Timothy 2:4:

"No man that warreth entangleth himself with the affairs of this life; that he may please him who hath chosen him to be a soldier."

When the battle is raging at the front lines, a soldier does not just go up to his captain and inform him that he has to quit fighting for a while because he has to go home and hoe his garden, or visit his grandmother, or take his girlfriend to the movies. Once committed to battle, a soldier must forget the business and social affairs of his life until the war is over. This is the example that Paul holds out to Timothy as a parallel for Christian service.

We next read 2 Timothy 2:5:

*"And if a man also strive for masteries, yet is
he not crowned, except he strive lawfully."*

If a runner in a race jumps the gun, or interferes
with another contestant, he is disqualified. If the horse
of a rodeo contestant leaves the stall too soon, no time
is allotted. If the lineman on a football team jumps
before the ball is snapped, or a man on the backfield is
illegally in motion, the team is penalized. In all
athletic contests there are rules to follow. Those who
break the rules usually do not win.

In the reference just alluded to, Paul had in mind
an athlete in the Greek olympic games. The crown, or
reward, for the winner was a wreath for the head
woven of ivy, roses, oak leaves, or some other plant
that had symbolic meaning. But the athletes in the
original olympic games had to not only obey the rules
governing the contest, but in order to insure the best
athletic ability in them, they had to live by rules
preceding the game. Any contestant competing was
required to train for ten months preceding the olympic
games. This training included living a separated life in
order to keep one's mind on the goal, and being placed
on a rigid diet. Should a Greek athlete break training
rules, he would be disqualified and be known as a
castaway. It was the training of a Grecian athlete, and
the rules governing the olympic games, that Paul had
in mind when he wrote: *"Know ye not that they which
run in a race run all, but one receiveth the prize? So
run, that ye may obtain. And every man that striveth*

for the mastery is temperate in all things. Now they do it to obtain a corruptible crown; but we an incorruptible. I therefore so run, not as uncertainly; so fight I, not as one that beateth the air: But I keep under my body, and bring it into subjection: lest that by any means, when I have preached to others, I myself should be a castaway" (1 Cor. 9:24-27).

Paul impressed upon Timothy (and the lesson is just as applicable to us), if a contestant in the olympic games would undergo all that strenuous training and self-discipline just for a chance to win a wreath of leaves that would be dead and gone in a day or two, then how much more should Christians be willing to train, work, and even suffer in order to win a reward of infinitely greater value — an incorruptible crown that will never fade or pass away.

"The husbandman that laboureth must be first partaker of the fruits" (2 Tim. 2:6).

In this verse Paul continues on the theme of diligence and dedication in Christian service. He gives as a first example a soldier, secondly an athlete, and thirdly a farmer. A similar pattern was established by Paul in 1 Corinthians 9:6-9: *"Or I only and Barnabas, have not we power to forbear working? Who goeth a warfare any time at his own charges? who planteth a vineyard, and eateth not of the fruit thereof? or who feedeth a flock, and eateth not of the milk of the flock? Say I these things as a man? or saith not the law the same also? For it is written in the law of Moses, Thou shalt not muzzle the mouth of the ox that treadeth out the corn. Doth God take care for oxen?"*

Under the law, the first fruits of the orchards, vineyards, or grain were to be given to the Lord. Then, the husbandman or farmer was entitled to the next fruits or harvest. Taking all three examples within the same context, Paul instructed Timothy in the matter of Christian service that it is better not to become entangled with the affairs of this life. When a minister or a missionary becomes involved in business, then he worries about it. His loyalties are divided. In several of his epistles, Paul alludes to his practice of working with his own hands to take care of his needs. In other places, he mentions receiving offerings from the churches. From Acts 18:3 we conclude that Paul worked most often at making tents, but in such cases (for example, at Thessalonica) he worked to provide for his needs when taking money from the church would bring scorn upon the gospel by unbelievers. But such cases are to be the exception rather than the rule. Those in God's service, like the athlete, should be able to put aside every weight and every care in order to give all of their time and energy to their calling in Christ Jesus.

Paul used a like example to impress upon the church at Jerusalem the importance of steady and consistent Christian service in Hebrews 12:1-2: *"Wherefore seeing we also are compassed about with so great a cloud of witnesses, let us lay aside every weight, and the sin which doth so easily beset us, and let us run with patience the race that is set before us, Looking unto Jesus the author and finisher of our faith; who for the joy that was set before him endured the cross, despising the shame, and is set down at the right hand of the throne of God."*

After pointing out to Timothy that there are times when Christians must be strong, and like soldiers, endure hard times, likewise they are to be firm, resolute, and steadfast when the occasion calls for it.

The apostle points out in 2 Timothy 2:7-13 that Christians must, at certain times and places, be ready to suffer for the gospel:

> *"Consider what I say; and the Lord give thee understanding in all things. Remember that Jesus Christ of the seed of David was raised from the dead according to my gospel: Wherein I suffer trouble, as an evil doer, even unto bonds; but the word of God is not bound. Therefore I endure all things for the elect's sake, that they may also obtain the salvation which is in Christ Jesus with eternal glory. It is a faithful saying: For if we be dead with him, we shall also live with him: If we suffer, we shall also reign with him: if we deny him, he also will deny us: If we believe not, yet he abideth faithful: he cannot deny himself."*

In verse seven, Paul informs Timothy that if some of the things in his letters are difficult to comprehend, just consider, or meditate upon them, and God will open his understanding as to their true meaning and application. Too often, Christians will read a difficult passage of Scripture, and then immediately close their Bible with the conviction that there is no way they can understand it. But God says to meditate upon the Word and pray, and the answer will come. We read in James 1:4-6: *"But let patience have her perfect work, that ye may be perfect and entire, wanting nothing. If any of you lack wisdom, let him ask of God, that giveth to all men liberally, and upbraideth not; and it shall be given him. But let him ask in faith, nothing wavering. For he that wavereth is like a wave of the sea driven with the wind and tossed."*

In verse eight, Paul instructs Timothy to remember, or always keep in mind, that Jesus Christ of the seed of David was raised from the dead. In the first chapter of Matthew the lineage of Jesus Christ is traced from Abraham, through David. Matthew deemed it important to list King David first as his father, "Jesus Christ, the son of David" (Matt. 1:1). As the son of David, Jesus Christ was the rightful heir to the throne of Israel. The angel announced to Mary, *"He shall be great, and shall be called the Son of the Highest: and the Lord God shall give unto him the throne of his father David"* (Luke 1:32). Matthew ends the lineage of David in Jesus Christ, stipulating that He is the end of the royal line and no one other than Jesus has the legal right to the throne. When Jesus presented Himself in Jerusalem to claim the throne, Israel shouted, ". . . *We will not have this man to reign over us"* (Luke 19:14). Subsequently, He was crucified at the request of the majority.

As long as the apostles and disciples preached that Jesus was a good man, a great teacher, a prophet, or a holy man of God, no one bothered them. But when they proclaimed that he arose from the dead, persecution came. This fact is stressed over and over in Acts and the epistles. For example, we read in Acts 5:29-33: *"Then Peter and the other apostles answered and said, We ought to obey God rather than men. The God of our fathers raised up Jesus, whom ye slew and hanged on a tree. Him hath God exalted with his right hand to be a Prince and a Saviour, for to give repentance to Israel, and forgiveness of sins. And we are his witnesses of these things; and so is also the Holy Ghost, whom God hath given to them that obey him. When they heard that, they were cut to the heart, and took counsel to slay them."*

Paul stressed that his main persecution came from preaching that Jesus Christ was raised from the dead. This kind of preaching greatly disturbed both the Jewish hierarchy and the Romans. It meant that Jesus, the apparent heir to the throne of Israel, was still alive. If alive, then He could return to claim it. Therefore, for preaching that Jesus Christ was raised from the dead, Paul said that he was charged as an evil *doer, and was in prison awaiting execution. But Paul had to preach the resurrection of Jesus, because if He was not raised as prophesied, then He was a false messiah and there was no atonement for sin. He established this principal precept in 1 Corinthians 15:12-18: "Now if Christ be preached that he rose from the dead, how say some among you that there is no resurrection of the dead? But if there be no resurrection of the dead, then is Christ not risen: And if Christ be not risen, then is our preaching vain, and your faith is also vain. Yea, and we are found false witnesses of God; because we have testified of God that he raised up Christ: whom he raised not up, if so be that the dead rise not. For if the dead rise not, then is not Christ raised: And if Christ be not raised, your faith is vain; ye are yet in your sins. Then they also which are fallen asleep in Christ are perished."*

As Dr. Bob Jones, Sr., used to say, "Any preaching that does not get Jesus Christ up out of the grave is not worth a hill of beans."

Therefore, Paul concluded that he preached Jesus, crucified for sins and raised again according to the will of God, so that the elect might obtain salvation. The elect referred to in 2 Timothy 2:10 are Christians — the saved of the dispensation of grace. Elect means to select or pick out for the fulfilling of a specific mission, or purpose.

Next, Paul lists four faithful sayings. At this time in the early history of the church, there were no copies of the New Testament. The three epistles of John and the Revelation had not even been written, and copies of the Pauline epistles were confined for the most part to the churches, or the individuals to whom they were sent. However, some of the preaching, or accounts of the life, death, and resurrection of Jesus by the apostles, and especially Paul, had been passed on and repeated until they became sayings, or memory verses. These four sayings were:

1. *"If we be dead with him, we shall live with him."* This saying could have been taken from Paul's letter to the Galatians, *"I am crucified with Christ: nevertheless I live; yet not I, but Christ liveth in me: and the life which I now live in the flesh I live by the faith of the Son of God, who loved me, and gave himself for me"* (Gal. 2:20). Or from Romans 6:8-11, *"Now if we be dead with Christ, we believe that we shall also live with him: Knowing that Christ being raised from the dead dieth no more; death hath no more dominion over him. For in that he died, he died unto sin once: but in that he liveth, he liveth unto God. Likewise reckon ye also yourselves to be dead indeed unto sin, but alive unto God through Jesus Christ our Lord."* When a man or woman accepts Jesus Christ as Savior, God reckons that person as dead to sin. But in that Jesus Christ was raised from the grave and lives, God also reckons the new Christian to likewise have risen to a new life in Christ. The body continues to decline and die, but the new man lives with eternal life.

2. *"If we suffer, we shall also reign with him."* There is a special reward for those who are called to suffer for Jesus. This reward is in the area of government. When the apostles reminded Jesus that they had forsaken everything for Him, He informed them that their reward would come in the Kingdom age when they would rule over the twelve tribes of Israel. Of those who give their lives for Jesus during the tribulation, we read in Revelation 20:4, *"And I saw thrones, and they sat upon them, and judgment was given unto them: and I saw the souls of them that were beheaded for the witness of Jesus, and for the word of God, and which had not worshipped the beast, neither his image, neither had received his mark upon their foreheads, or in their hands; and they lived and reigned with Christ a thousand years."* When Jesus Christ returns, He will establish His own government, as is declared in Isaiah 9:6-7: *"For unto us a child is born, unto us a son is given: and the government shall be upon his shoulder: and his name shall be called Wonderful, Counsellor, The mighty God, The everlasting Father, The Prince of Peace. Of the increase of his government and peace there shall be no end, upon the throne of David, and upon his kingdom, to order it, and to establish it with judgment and with justice from henceforth even for ever."* The thrones of Revelation 20:4 will be for those who have suffered and died for Jesus Christ. Among these will be the apostles, the tribulation martyrs, and all those mentioned by

Paul in 2 Timothy 2:9. We read also in Romans 8:17-18, *"And if children, then heirs; heirs of God, and joint-heirs with Christ; if so be that we suffer with him, that we may be also glorified together. For I reckon that the sufferings of this present time are not worthy to be compared with the glory which shall be revealed in us."*

3. *"If we deny him, he also will deny us."* The nation of Israel denied Jesus as charged by Peter, *"The God of Abraham, and of Isaac, and of Jacob, the God of our fathers, hath glorified his Son Jesus; whom ye delivered up, and denied him in the presence of Pilate, when he was determined to let him go. But ye denied the Holy One and the Just, and desired a murderer to be granted unto you"* (Acts 3:13-14). Peter himself had previously denied Jesus three times (John 13:38). Peter, however, repented and received forgiveness from the Lord, and became a leading defender of the faith. In the day when Paul wrote his epistle to Timothy, a Christian who was arrested would first be given an opportunity to recant and deny Jesus Christ as his Lord and Savior. If he refused, then he was usually executed.

"When he was brought to the tribunal, there was a great tumult as soon as it was generally understood that Polycarp was apprehended. The proconsul asked him if he were Polycarp. When he assented, the former counselled him to deny Christ, saying, 'Consider thyself, and have pity on thy own great age'; and many other such-like speeches which

they are wont to make — 'Swear, by the fortune of Caesar' — 'Repent.' . . . The proconsul then urged him, saying, 'Swear, and I will release thee; reproach Christ.' Polycarp answered, 'Eighty and six years have I served him, and he never once wronged me; how then shall I blaspheme my King, Who hath saved me?' . . . 'I will tame thee with fire,' said the proconsul, 'since you despise the wild beasts, unless you repent.' Then said Polycarp, 'You threaten me with fire, which burns for an hour and is soon extinguished; but the fire of the future judgment, and of eternal punishment reserved for the ungodly, you are ignorant of. But why do you delay? Do whatever you please.' "(taken from *Foxes Book Of Martyrs*).

Polycarp was then bound, placed on a pile of wood, and burned.

Hundreds of thousands of Christians have been fed to the lions, crucified, beheaded, or burned at the stake for refusing to deny Jesus Christ as Lord and Savior. Those who denied Jesus Christ may not have been born again in the first place. This point can be argued; nevertheless, they were certainly not known as Christians after the public denial. Before the world, God has ultimately given them up so that the name of Christ will not be disgraced, thus preventing men and women from coming to the knowledge of the truth and being saved.

4. *"If we believe not, yet he abideth faithful: he cannot deny himself."* Paul wrote in 1 Corinthians 12:12,

27, *"For as the body is one, and hath many members, and all the members of that one body, being many, are one body: so also is Christ . . . Now ye are the body of Christ, and members in particular."* While Jesus Christ will deny those who are not His, He cannot deny those who truly belong to Him. All born-again believers, Christians in spirit as well as name, belong to the body of Christ. To cut them off would be to cut off His own body; to deny them would be to deny Himself. Even though Christians may be unfaithful, Jesus is faithful to save all who come to Him in faith.

We continue now with 2 Timothy 2:14-16:

"Of these things put them in remembrance, charging them before the Lord that they strive not about words to no profit, but to the subverting of the hearers. Study to shew thyself approved unto God, a workman that needeth not to be ashamed, rightly dividing the word of truth. But shun profane and vain babblings: for they will increase unto more ungodliness."

In this portion of the second chapter, Paul gives Timothy four commands:

1. *Remind men of these basic doctrinal truths;* like children, the Christian's attention span is often

short-lived. Sound doctrine must become the basis for every message, for every teaching, and for every sermon. The problem with so many of the churches and denominations today is that vague philosophies and social gospel theory have replaced the central theme of the Bible — the death, burial, resurrection, and return of Jesus Christ as the hope of this present world. Consequently, as Paul warned, false cults have stolen away the weak in faith.

2. *Charge Christians not to contend about words to no profit.* There is nothing wrong with going back to the Greek and Hebrew texts to better define the meaning of certain words in the Scriptures. However, many make a mockery of word definition. They will take a single word out of context, explain it according to the Greek meaning, and then start an entirely new doctrine from the definition of one word. The liberals and apostates also get in on the word definition game. They may contend that where the Bible speaks of the resurrection of Jesus, the word "resurrection" really does not mean that Jesus was raised from the dead, but that He lives in our hearts. For example, it is impossible to rightly explain the meaning of the word "love" if taken out of context. Some men love money; some love drugs; some love their wives, etc. Definitions of words must be arrived at only within the context of the subject. Paul warns Timothy not to let the congregation become embroiled in arguments over words, phrases, or even verses that will lead to the subverting

of the faith of the members.

3. *Like a laborer who proves his own ability through his works, study to become an approved minister of the gospel.* A man may tell you he is a good carpenter, and may even convince you that he is vastly experienced, but not until he finishes building your house will you know for sure. A Christian may talk well, but unless he has the right tool — a comprehensive knowledge of the Word of God — and then becomes experienced in applying it in actual service, he cannot rightly be approved as a minister, evangelist, teacher, or soul winner. Without a sound biblical background, a Christian cannot rightly divide the Scriptures. For instance, God told Noah to build an ark, but that does not mean He commands us all to go out and build an ark. There can be no substitute for Bible study and sound instructions.

4. *Shun, or reject, vain or meaningless babblings.* The word "vain" as used here means words that the speaker uses to build himself up and to show how much he knows rather than what God has given him. These are words spoken in self-pride. I am sure that most have listened to sermons where the speakers used flowery terminology and big words, and afterward, you may say it was certainly a great message, but that you have no idea what it was about, or the purpose for which it was given. Paul indicates that such men use these vain babblings to cover up false doctrines.

We continue and read 2 Timothy 2:17-18:

"And their word will eat as doth a canker: of whom is Hymenaeus and Philetus; Who concerning the truth have erred, saying that the resurrection is past already; and overthrow the faith of some"

False doctrine is like a cancer. Just as cancer will grow and spread throughout the body until it takes the life of the victim, false doctrine will destroy the hope of eternal life through Christ in the lives of believers. Nothing is known about Hymenaeus and Philetus except they were false teachers. Like all such men, they did not go outside the church and establish their own congregation. They subverted the faith of their fellow church members, and started a false cult. Paul did not reveal what Bible truth they perverted. It could have been the incident recorded in Matthew 27:51-53: *"And, behold, the veil of the temple was rent in twain from the top to the bottom; and the earth did quake, and the rocks rent; And the graves were opened; and many bodies of the saints which slept arose, And came out of the graves after his resurrection, and went into the holy city, and appeared unto many."* Their teaching that the resurrection was past left no hope for the future resurrection for those who died in Christ.

"Nevertheless the foundation of God standeth

sure, having this seal, The Lord knoweth them that are his. And, Let every one that nameth the name of Christ depart from iniquity" (2 Tim. 2:19).

Regardless of how the winds of false doctrine assail the Word of God, His foundation remains unshakable. The Lord knows those who have believed unto salvation, and we are to hold fast to the truth of 1 Thessalonians 4:16-17: *"For the Lord himself shall descend from heaven with a shout, with the voice of the archangel, and with the trump of God: and the dead in Christ shall rise first: Then we which are alive and remain shall be caught up together with them in the clouds, to meet the Lord in the air: and so shall we ever be with the Lord."*

Continuing, we read 2 Timothy 2:20-21:

"But in a great house there are not only vessels of gold and of silver, but also of wood and of earth; and some to honour, and some to dishonour. If a man therefore purge himself from these, he shall be a vessel unto honour, sanctified, and meet for the master's use, and prepared unto every good work."

In the preceding verse Paul made reference to the one true church, the body of all born-again believers, when he wrote, "the Lord knoweth them that are his." In verses twenty and twenty-one, he speaks of the visible church, the local church, or of all the people belonging to a church, or a collection of churches. He said that in this great, all inclusive household, there are some vessels that bring honor to the Lord of the house — vessels of gold and silver. Also, there are some vessels that bring no honor, or prestige, or glory to Him — vessels of wood and earth. In the Oriental world, vessels were, and still are, of great importance. Beautiful plates, bowls, or urns of gold and silver were proudly displayed and used to serve important guests. But the vessels used to wash feet in, or laundry, were made of wood or clay. To make a modern application, a proud housewife would not have a garbage can on her coffee table. The overall application goes back to the preceding verses where the apostle speaks of those who remain faithful and godly in testimony and service, in contrast to those who give themselves to vain babblings and false doctrines. Therefore, believers are exhorted to purge themselves, or separate themselves from the wood and the clay so that they may be vessels like unto gold and silver that will bring honor to Jesus Christ. Christians are commanded to be sanctified, which means simply to be set apart wholly for the service of God. It is interesting that Paul used the same terminology in reference to works and rewards in 1 Corinthians 3:11-15: *"For other foundation can no man lay than that is laid, which is Jesus Christ. Now if any man build upon this foundation gold, silver, precious stones, wood, hay, stubble; Every man's work shall be made manifest: for the day shall declare it, because it shall be revealed by fire; and the fire shall try every man's work of what sort it is. If any man's work abide which he hath built thereupon, he shall receive a reward. If any man's work shall be burned, he shall suffer loss: but he himself shall be saved; yet so as by fire."*

"Flee also youthful lusts: but follow righteousness, faith, charity, peace, with them that call on the Lord out of a pure heart" (2 Tim. 2:22).

Whether Paul's reference to youthful lusts was meant for Timothy specifically or whether it was simply a general reference meant for all young people in the church may be a matter of opinion or interpretation. Although Timothy must have been at least thirty-five years of age at the time of the writing of this epistle, he was still a young man to Paul as he makes mention of Timothy's youth in several verses. Without doubt, youthful lusts means immoral conduct. Only those who can call out to God in prayer out of a pure heart can truly seek His will in faith and peace. Sin in a Christian's life, and especially sin that results from lusts of the flesh, prevents God's children from boldly coming before the throne of grace. This same admonition was given by Paul to the church at Philippi: *"And the peace of God, which passeth all understanding, shall keep your hearts and minds through Christ Jesus. Finally, brethren, whatsoever*

things are true, whatsoever things are honest, what-
soever things are just, whatsoever things are pure,
whatsoever things are lovely, whatsoever things are of
good report; if there be any virtue, and if there be any
praise, think on these things" (Phil. 4:7-8). We are to
pursue, and keep our thoughts on things that are pure
before God. If we do this, then we have peace with
God and peace in our souls.

We next read 2 Timothy 2:23:

"But foolish and unlearned questions avoid,
knowing that they do gender strifes."

Paul gave Timothy a word of caution about
attempting to answer foolish, unlearned questions.
The Greek text means literally studid and childish
queries posed by those who are simply attempting to
stir up trouble or strife within the church. To deal with
such people and try to answer their questions would
create more problems and contentions, and encourage
more silly questions that would lead them further
from God's Word. Timothy is warned not to give any
credence to them, or to just ignore them. We read in
Proverbs 26:4, *"Answer not a fool according to his*
folly, lest thou also be like unto him."

We complete our study of the second chapter by
reading 2 Timothy 2:24-26:

"And the servant of the Lord must not
strive; but be gentle unto all men, apt to

*teach, patient, In meekness instructing those
that oppose themselves; if God peradventure
will give them repentance to the acknowledging of the truth; And that they may recover
themselves out of the snare of the devil, who
are taken captive by him at his will."*

These three verses are addressed to the servants
of the Lord. Within the context of this pastoral
epistle, it means those in God's service, or ministers
and teachers in the churches. God's servants in the
church must always avoid strife and teach and
minister to the members with patience, not being
overly judgmental with harsh rebukes. To make a
blanket condemnation without an expression of
genuine love for the one who has fallen into temptation
may drive him further away from fellowship with the
brethren. Therefore, Paul instructs Timothy to be
skilled in teaching and correcting those who have
erred so that they may repent, recover, and return to
the church. They are to be given every opportunity to
escape out of the snare of the devil.

However, there comes a time when all efforts to
restore such wayward Christians have been exhausted,
then stern measures are justified. For example, Paul
wrote to Titus, ". . . *The Cretians are always liars, evil
beasts, slow bellies. This witness is true. Wherefore
rebuke them sharply, that they may be sound in the
faith"* (Tit. 1:12-13). Also Paul, in reference to those in
the church at Corinth who steadfastly continued in

their licentious and ungodly ways, wrote: *"In the name of our Lord Jesus Christ, when ye are gathered together, and my spirit, with the power of our Lord Jesus Christ, To deliver such an one unto Satan for the destruction of the flesh, that the spirit may be saved in the day of the Lord Jesus"* (1 Cor. 5:4-5).

How to deal with carnal and wayward Christians was a great problem in the early churches just as it has been ever since, and as Paul wrote to Timothy, it requires much love, patience, and skill. The general rule is given in Galatians 6:1, *"Brethren, if a man be overtaken in a fault, ye which are spiritual, restore such an one in the spirit of meekness; considering thyself, lest thou also be tempted."*

The important thing for all to remember is that the blood of Jesus Christ can cleanse us from all sin. *". . . if we walk in the light, as he is in the light, we have fellowship one with another, and the blood of Jesus Christ his Son cleanseth us from all sin. If we say that we have no sin, we deceive ourselves, and the truth is not in us. If we confess our sins, he is faithful and just to forgive us our sins, and to cleanse us from all unrighteousness"* (1 John 1:7-9).

Chapter Three

At the close of the second chapter, Paul had written to Timothy concerning carnal Christians, immorality, false doctrines, and departing from the faith. In the third chapter, he uses these things as a sign of a greater apostasy at the end of the age. We begin by reading 2 Timothy 3:1-9:

"This know also, that in the last days perilous times shall come. For men shall be lovers of their own selves, covetous, boasters, proud, blasphemers, disobedient to parents, unthankful, unholy, Without natural affection, trucebreakers, false accusers, incontinent, fierce, despisers of those that are good, Traitors, heady, highminded, lovers of pleasures more than lovers of God; Having a form of godliness, but denying the power thereof: from such turn away. For of this sort are they which creep into houses, and lead captive silly women laden with sins, led away with divers lusts, Ever learning, and never able to come to the knowledge of the truth. Now as Jannes and Jambres withstood Moses, so do these also resist the truth: men

of corrupt minds, reprobate concerning the faith. But they shall proceed no further: for their folly shall be manifest unto all men, as their's also was."

The Greek word for perilous could also be interpreted troublesome, grievous, or hard. There are some who interpret last days to mean the entire span of time from the first advent of Christ to the second advent. However, it is our understanding that the last days refer to the end of the age only. Because this sign is given to the church, Paul doubtless meant the days just preceding the rapture. We quote from *The Pastoral Epistles In the Greek New Testament* by Dr. Kenneth Wuest:

"The expression 'in the last days,' refers to the time immediately preceding the rapture of the church and the second advent of the Lord Jesus. 'Times' is kairos, *which Trench defines as follows: 'a critical, epoch-making period foreordained of God when all that has been slowly, and often without observation, ripening through long ages, is mature and comes to the birth in grand decisive events, which constitute at once the close of one period and the commencement of another.' . . . The word speaks of difficult, dangerous times which Christians, living just before the rapture, will encounter."*

In the Bible there are fourteen different expressions used for the end of the age. I believe it would be good for all Christians to acquaint themselves with these various terms. Five of the most common are:

1. *Latter Times* — There are many definitions for time, or times, but the one given in *Webster's New World Dictionary* that best defines "latter times" is: *"a period of history, characterized by a given social structure; . . . prevailing conditions, past, present, or future, as times are bad."* When the expression "latter times" is found in the Bible, it means the time just preceding the return of Jesus Christ, and as indicated in 1 Timothy 4:1, includes the time preceding the rapture: *"Now the Spirit speaketh expressly, that in the latter times some shall depart from the faith, giving heed to seducing spirits, and doctrines of devils."*

2. *Latter Years* — This is an Old Testament term referring to the years between the time Israel would be refounded as a nation and the coming of the Messiah to bring in the Kingdom age. Israel today is living in the latter years, and we read of the coming invasion of Israel by Gog, or Russia, in Ezekiel 38:8: *"After many days thou shalt be visited: in the latter years thou shalt come into the land that is brought back from the sword, and is gathered out of many people, against the mountains of Israel, which have been always waste: but it is brought forth out of the nations, and they shall*

dwell safely all of them."

3. *Latter Days* — The term "latter days" as opposed to the term "latter years" would signify a shorter length of time. Therefore, the "latter days" usually refer to the very extremity of the age, the tribulation period. Concerning the revived Roman Empire and its destruction as the Antichrist's kingdom with the second coming of Jesus Christ, we read in Daniel 2:28: *"But there is a God in heaven that revealeth secrets, and maketh known to the king Nebuchadnezzar what shall be in the latter days. . . ."* In Ezekiel 38:16, the invasion is pinpointed further: *"And thou shalt come up against my people of Israel, as a cloud to cover the land; it shall be in the latter days. . . ."* We favor the position that the invasion of Israel by Russia will be soon after the rapture.

4. *Latter Day* — The "latter day" as opposed to "latter days" has reference to the millennium — the one thousand-year reign of Jesus Christ on David's throne. We read in Job 19:25, *"For I know that my redeemer liveth, and that he shall stand at the latter day upon the earth."*

5. *The Last Day* — This time speaks to us of the day of resurrection. For example, we read in John 6:40, *"And this is the will of him that sent me, that every one which seeth the Son, and believeth on him, may have everlasting life: and I will raise him up at the last day."* In the sixth chapter of John, the resurrection of the saved is spoken of as being "at

the last day," never *in* the last day, or *on* the last day. The last day also refers to the millennium, the rapture of the church, and the resurrection of the tribulation saints, which will follow seven years later.

Some contend that no prophetic sign is given to the church in all the Bible; therefore, Christians are not to be concerned about the signs of the times, or to study Bible prophecy. They conclude that no prophecy is being fulfilled today. We take the opposing view. We believe that scores of prophecies are being fulfilled right before our eyes. In 2 Timothy 3, Paul, by inspiration of God, wrote about an event that Christians should watch for in the last days — runaway humanism, materialism, and self-exultation. There are thirty evil characteristics of men in the last days. They are:

1. *Lovers of themselves* — selfish; thinking only of themselves.
2. *Covetous* — the Greek here indicates a love of money; making money the goal of their lives.
3. *Boasters* — braggarts; puffing themselves up before others.
4. *Proud* — taking pride in their own education, property, and accomplishments, while giving neither God, their family, nor their fellow man any credit.
5. *Blasphemers* — speaking evil of God and those things which are sacred before God.

6. *Disobedient to parents* — headstrong children, unmindful, disrespectful, and impossible to control.

7. *Unthankful* — while having an abundant material estate, they never take time to thank God; others think the world owes them a living.

8. *Unholy* — having no reverence for God, the Bible, or the church.

9. *Without natural affection* — a state of sinful, unnatural living; perverts and homosexuals.

10. *Trucebreakers* — the word used here in the Greek means "a libation," or a drink offering, that accompanied the making of treaties. The meaning is that men would rather be at war than at peace.

11. *False accusers* — slanderers, making libelous accusations against others.

12. *Incontinent* — no control of appetites, lusts, and passions.

13. *Fierce* — uncivilized, wild in appearance, and animal-like in conduct.

14. *Despisers of good men* — hating those who try to live godly lives.

15. *Traitors* — betrayers of friends and country; having no loyalty.

16. *Heady* — headstrong; not listening to reason.

17. *Highminded* — conceited; having a false sense of importance.

18. *Lovers of pleasure more than lovers of God* — caring more for recreation than for doing God's service.

19. *Having a form of godliness* — pretending to be

godly with a profession of words, perhaps even going to church, yet living ungodly lives.

20. *Denying the power of God* — professing a belief in God, yet denying that God has power in this present world to change lives or world events.

21. *Using a religious front to deceive others* — Pretending to be ministers, they use the Christian name for their own selfish interests.

22. *Deceivers of silly women* — Some use their position to enhance their relations with women.

23. *Ever learning but never coming to the knowledge of the truth* — willing to pursue knowledge of false science or false religions, yet spending no time learning about the truth of God.

24. *Stubbornly resist the truth* — like Jannes and Jambres withstood Moses, so do these men stand against God's true servants today.

25. *Corrupt minds* — Jesus said that like it was in the days of Noah, so it would be again. *"And God saw that the wickedness of man was great in the earth, and that every imagination of the thoughts of his heart was only evil continually"* (Gen. 6:5).

26. *Reprobates* — The dictionary provides the description, *"depraved; vicious; unprincipled. In theology, rejected by God; excluded from salvation and lost in sin."*

27. *Evil* — morally bad, wicked; servants of the devil causing pain, sorrow, and trouble.

28. *Seducers* — those who have as their primary objective in life the pursuit of fornication and

adultery.

29. *Waxing worse and worse* — the primary meaning of wax is to weave. Therefore, by design they continually add to their state of reprobation.

30. *Deceivers* — a deceiver is someone who gains the confidence of others and then misleads them into believing that the false is reality; that a lie is the truth.

Thus, we conclude Paul's checklist for moral behavior and conduct in the last days. This does not mean that everyone has these bad and evil qualities; but rather that, as the end of the age winds down, the general populace becomes more and more like the Antediluvian society. As we watch television news programs, read our daily newspapers, and observe the latest crime statistics, we can conclude that we are indeed living in those perilous times which Paul alluded to in his second epistle to Timothy.

Thirty is the biblical number for maturity. We see, in these thirty attributes of wickedness that which will prevail in the last days, the fullness or maturity that Paul spoke about in 2 Thessalonians 2:3-12: *Let no man deceive you by any means: for that day shall not come, except there come a falling away first, and that man of sin be revealed, the son of perdition; Who opposeth and exalteth himself above all that is called God, or that is worshipped; so that he as God sitteth in the temple of God, shewing himself that he is God. Remember ye not, that, when I was yet with you, I told you these things? And now ye know what withholdeth that he might be revealed in his time. For the mystery of iniquity doth already work: only he who now letteth will let, until he be taken out of the way. And then shall that Wicked be revealed, whom the Lord shall consume with the spirit of his mouth, and shall destroy with the brightness of his coming: Even him, whose coming is after the working of Satan with all power and signs and lying wonders, And with all deceivableness of unrighteousness in them that perish; because they received not the love of the truth, that they might be saved. And for this cause God shall send them strong delusion, that they should believe a lie: That they all might be damned who believed not the truth, but had pleasure in unrighteousness."*

It will be the consummation of wickedness and a rejection of God that will make it possible for the Antichrist, a man who is so evil that he is called the "man of sin," to become the world dictator. It is therefore no wonder that when the mass iniquity that Paul wrote to Timothy about becomes prevalent in the last days, the great majority of the human race will worship this Antichrist as their god. This most important sign that Paul gave to the church in the last days is certainly in evidence today.

Paul wrote to Timothy in his second epistle that in the last days there would be a form of godliness, but the inward nature of the people themselves would be ungodly. As we look at our own nation today, we see an outward church structure — thousands of churches with large memberships. Yet, when we get beneath this outward form, we find selfishness, greed, lust, homosexuality, traitors, blasphemers, murder, teenage criminals, robbers, pornography, alcoholism, and drug addiction. But this is just one of the many signs of the last days that is given in the Bible.

We understand that the church is not given the sign of the Antichrist standing in the Temple, the battle of Armageddon, or Jesus Christ coming with the armies of Heaven to destroy the armies of Antichrist. However, Christians are given many signs relating to these events so that we can know from the abundance of connecting circumstantial evidence that the coming of the Lord is near. Jesus said in Matthew 24:32-33: *"Now learn a parable of the fig tree; When his branch is yet tender, and putteth forth leaves, ye know that summer is nigh: So likewise ye, when ye shall see all these things, know that it is near, even at the doors."*

We think the fig tree is representative of the refounding of Israel as a nation. But regardless of whether this is the case or not, the statement that Jesus made still stands. When people living in the last generation "see all these things" that Jesus prophesied would come to pass, then they are to know that His coming is near. The things that Jesus said the last generation should look for are all prophecies from Matthew 24:5-34. He introduced these prophecies with the words, *". . . Take heed that no man deceive you"* (Matt. 24:4). Jesus indicated quite plainly that all these prophecies were not to come to pass in a day, a month, a year, or seven years. They were to be fulfilled over a period of a generation.

Jesus also said in Luke 21:28, *"And when these things begin to come to pass, then look up, and lift up your heads; for your redemption draweth nigh."* Again, our Lord said that the prophecy that would herald His coming again could not be fulfilled in a day, a month, a year, or seven years. This truth is also explained in Luke 21:31-32, *"So likewise ye, when ye see these things come to pass, know ye that the kingdom of God is nigh at hand. Verily I say unto you, This generation shall not pass away, till all be fulfilled."* Again we see the time period set forth by Jesus — a generation. Inasmuch as we believe the Bible indicates the church will be raptured just seven years before Christ's return, Christians living in the last days will witness the fulfillment of many prophecies that precede the coming of the Lord. Prophetic signs that Christians can discern, and relate to the return of Jesus Christ for His church are as follows:

- Increase of knowledge (Dan. 12:4).
- Rise in the speed of travel and communications (Dan. 12:4).
- The rise of Russia as a great power which will invade Israel (Ezek. 38).
- The development of weapons capable of destroying entire nations in an hour (Ezek. 29:9-12; Rev. 8:7).
- Signs in the heavens (Isa. 30:26; Joel 2:30-31; Matt.

24:29; Rev. 8:12).
- The re-establishment of Israel as a nation (Isa. 43:5-6; Hos. 8:8-10; Amos 9:11-15; Luke 24:24; Acts 15:16).
- Increase in earthquakes (Matt. 24:7).
- Wars of worldwide proportions (Matt. 24:7).
- The rise of false messiahs and false prophets (Matt. 24:24).
- Fear of mass destruction (Luke 24:26).
- The rebuilding of Babylon (Jer. 51:52; Isa. 13:19-20; Rev. 18).
- Increase of lawlessness (Matt. 24:12; 2 Thess. 2:7; 2 Tim. 3:1-9).
- Apostasy within the church (1 Tim. 4:1-2; 2 Tim. 4:3; Rev. 3:14-18).
- Preparations for the restoration of Jewish sacrificial worship (Dan. 12:11; Matt. 24:15; 2 Thess. 2:3-4).

There are many other prophecies, though not given specifically to the church. Christians can know from developments leading to their fulfillment that these prophecies are also near fulfillment. In Revelation 6:6, world inflation is indicated, and in Revelation 13, a new economic order is revealed where everyone will be commanded to work, buy, and sell using code marks and numbers. Also, in Zechariah 14:2, Daniel 12:1, and Revelation 19, it is prophesied that before the Lord returns, all nations will be against Israel. Christians can see the evidence of these prophecies being fulfilled within the next few years.

We continue in our study and read 2 Timothy 3:10-11:

> *"But thou hast fully known my doctrine, manner of life, purpose, faith, longsuffering, charity, patience, Persecutions, afflictions, which came unto me at Antioch, at Iconium, at Lystra; what persecutions I endured: but out of them all the Lord delivered me."*

In these verses Paul lists nine things by which a Christian can measure his witness for the Lord Jesus Christ:

1. *Doctrine* — Everyone, by Paul's preaching, knew exactly what he believed about the Word of God, the atoning death of Jesus Christ, His resurrection, and His return. He spoke in simple and plain terms so that there could be no doubt in anyone's mind about God's plan of salvation. He wrote in Romans 16:17-18, *"Now I beseech you, brethren, mark them which cause divisions and offences contrary to the doctrine which ye have learned; and avoid them. For they that are such serve not our Lord Jesus Christ, but their own belly; and by good words and fair speeches deceive the hearts of the simple."*

2. *Manner of life* — Paul did not preach one thing and do another. He lived by the Christian standards he advocated for others. He wrote in Philippians 2:14-15, *"Do all things without murmurings and*

disputings: That ye may be blameless and harmless, the sons of God, without rebuke, in the midst of a crooked and perverse nation, among whom ye shine as lights in the world."

3. *Faith* — No one ever doubted Paul's faith. If he ever doubted his calling, his salvation, and the message which God gave him to proclaim for the Gentiles, it was not revealed in any of his epistles. In Ephesians 4:5-6, he wrote, *"One Lord, one faith, one baptism, One God and Father of all, who is above all, and through all, and in you all."*

4. *Longsuffering* — He suffered often, but never wavered. His longsuffering is declared in Philippians 3:8, *"Yea doubtless, and I count all things but loss for the excellency of the knowledge of Christ Jesus my Lord: for whom I have suffered the loss of all things, and do count them but dung, that I may win Christ."*

5. *Charity* — The word here again means God's love. Wherever he went, Paul shed the love of God abroad to all men. He wrote in Romans 13:8, *"Owe no man any thing, but to love one another. . . ."* The debt that Paul felt he owed to every man was to let them know that God loved them and sent His Son, Jesus Christ, to die for them.

6. *Purpose* — There was never any doubt in Paul's mind as to why he gave up all things for Jesus Christ. The purpose of his ministry was clearly presented through his words and his life. He wrote in 1 Corinthians 9:22, *". . . I am made all things to*

all men, that I might by all means save some."

7. *Patience* — Patience here means steadfastness. In spite of all the things which Paul had to endure and suffer for the gospel's sake, he never gave up or wavered. He just kept doing what he thought God expected him to do.

8. *Persecutions* — *Webster's New World Dictionary* gives the following definition for persecute: *"To afflict or harass constantly so as to injure or distress; oppress cruelly, especially for religious reasons."* Paul was constantly beset and harassed for the preaching of the gospel, yet he never let these persecutions deter him from his mission.

9. *Afflictions* — The meaning of affliction is very similar to the meaning for persecution. *Webster's New World Dictionary* gives the following definition: *"An afflicted condition; pain, suffering, or distress imposed by illness, loss, or misfortune."* The afflictions endured by Paul for the gospel not only included the beatings, stonings, and imprisonments that he suffered, but also the hunger, shipwrecks, and other misfortunes which he encountered.

These nine things that Paul said about his ministry were not for the purpose of boasting, but rather to give Timothy guidelines that he might follow. Paul knew that he was about to be executed; therefore, the burden of looking over the churches and contending for the faith would fall upon Timothy.

Therefore, Paul in this part of his letter encourages Timothy to follow in his footsteps so that the gospel committed to him by Jesus Christ would continue doctrinally pure, so that souls would continue to be saved and added to the church.

> *"Yea, and all that live godly in Christ Jesus shall suffer persecution. But evil men and seducers shall wax worse and worse, deceiving, and being deceived"* (2 Tim. 3:12-13).

It is a basic truth that Christians who live godly lives will at some time suffer persecution. It may be from a neighbor, a friend, a loved one, or a stranger. Jesus said in John 15:18-19, *"If the world hate you, ye know that it hated me before it hated you. If ye were of the world, the world would love his own: but because ye are not of the world, but I have chosen you out of the world, therefore the world hateth you."*

Paul, and many others of the early Christian church, suffered persecutions almost every day. In the United States, and generally in the identified Free World, Christians may not suffer governmental persecution, at least at this time. In Russia, however, and in mainland China as well, Christians have been called to suffer persecution, and even martyrdom. The reference to "evil men and seducers waxing worse and worse, deceiving and being deceived," leads ultimately to the last days. In his first letter to Timothy, Paul wrote, *"Now the Spirit speaketh expressly, that in the latter times some shall depart from the faith, giving heed to seducing spirits, and doctrines of devils; Speaking lies in hypocrisy; having their conscience seared with a hot iron"* (1 Tim. 4:1-2). In 2 Thessalonians 2:10-11, the same prophecy is presented, *"And with all deceivableness of unrighteousness in them that perish; because they received not the love of the truth, that they might be saved. And for this cause God shall send them strong delusion, that they should believe a lie."* We are indeed living in the latter times when evil men and seducers are waxing worse and worse.

> *"But continue thou in the things which thou hast learned and hast been assured of, knowing of whom thou hast learned them; And that from a child thou hast known the holy scriptures, which are able to make thee wise unto salvation through faith which is in Christ Jesus"* (2 Tim. 3:14-15).

In these two verses, Paul exhorts Timothy to continue in the things that he had learned, always keeping in mind that they were committed to him first by his mother, and then by the Apostle Paul who received the gospel directly from Jesus Christ. As soon as Timothy was old enough to understand spiritual truths, his mother read to him the books of the Old Testament. This was the Septuagint that had the books of Moses, the prophets, and the Psalms, in one volume. When Timothy was a boy, there were no books of the New Testament in print. However, from the Old Testament the prophecies concerning the coming Messiah had been read to him, and when Paul presented Jesus Christ to him as that Messiah promised by the prophets, he believed and was saved. The Old Testament can make a person wise unto salvation by pointing the way to Jesus Christ, but salvation comes only by faith in Jesus Christ who came to die in the sinner's place.

We next read 2 Timothy 3:16-17:

"All scripture is given by inspiration of God, and is profitable for doctrine, for reproof, for correction, for instruction in righteousness: That the man of God may be perfect, throughly furnished unto all good works."

Although the books of the Bible reveal the personality and identity of the authors, the words are the result of the Holy Spirit directing the minds of these men. The Scriptures, therefore, are the very Word of God. There is a central theme revealing the whole purpose of God in sending His Son to save lost humanity. Also within the Scriptures there is a numerical pattern as well as a prophetic correlation that proves beyond doubt that the authors, living over a time span of two thousand years, could not possibly have written all sixty-six books through their own understanding or design. The writers themselves bear testimony that they were directed by God to write as He dictated.

For example, the prophet wrote in Ezekiel 1:3, *"The word of the Lord came expressly unto Ezekiel. . . ."* Almost every chapter in Ezekiel begins, "And the word of the Lord came unto me, saying." The authors felt they were under a burden until the words they received from God were written. We read in Zechariah 9:1, *"The burden of the word of the Lord in the land of Hadrach. . . ."* The last book of the Old Testament begins, *"The burden of the word of the Lord to Israel by Malachi"* (Mal. 1:1).

The New Testament books were added to the Old Testament because they too were inspired by God. The writers who walked with Jesus were led by the Holy Spirit to put on parchment the miracles, words, and events surrounding Christ's earthly ministry. For example, we read in John 14:26, *"But the Comforter, which is the Holy Ghost, whom the Father will send in my name, he shall teach you all things, and bring all things to your remembrance, whatsoever I have said unto you."*

The Apostle Paul was moved by divine revelation in writing fourteen books of the New Testament. He wrote to the church at Ephesus, *"For this cause I Paul, the prisoner of Jesus Christ for you Gentiles, If ye have heard of the dispensation of the grace of God which is given me to you-ward: How that by revelation he made known unto me the mystery . . ."* (Eph. 3:1-3). He also stated in 1 Corinthians 14:37, *"If any man think himself to be a prophet, or spiritual, let him acknowledge that the things that I write unto you are the commandments of the Lord."*

In the first book of the Bible we read the words "And God said" over and over again. In the last book of the Bible we read, *"The Revelation of Jesus Christ, which God gave unto him, to shew unto his servants things which must shortly come to pass; and he sent and signified it by his angel unto his servant John: Who bare record of the word of God . . ."* (Rev. 1:1-2).

Paul, in all confidence, could write, *"All scripture is given by inspiration of God, and is profitable for doctrine, for reproof, for correction, for instruction in righteousness: That the man of God may be perfect, throughly furnished unto all good works"* (2 Tim. 3:16-17).

As we see so-called ministers of God today debating over whether the Bible is fallible or infallible, the Word of God or the words of men, we know that we are truly living in the days prophesied by Paul in 2 Timothy 4:3-4, *". . . the time will come when they will not endure sound doctrine; but after their own lusts shall they heap to themselves teachers, having itching ears; And they shall turn away their ears from the truth, and shall be turned unto fables."*

Paul declares that *all* Scripture is given by inspiration of God — not just part, not fifty percent, not ninety percent, not even ninety-nine percent, but every word!

Let us now examine what Paul said of the Scriptures as pertaining to ministers, teachers, evangelists, and all others in Christian service:

1. *Profitable for doctrine* — to convince men of the truth of God and His way of salvation.
2. *Profitable for teaching* — to teach believers about God and His will for their lives.
3. *Profitable for reproof* — use the Scriptures to expose to Christians those things they do that bring discredit upon the name of Jesus Christ.
4. *Profitable for correction* — to show Christians the error of false doctrines and teachings and restore them to the way of faith and truth.
5. *Profitable for instruction in righteousness* — the Scriptures are not only for showing men and women what they should not do, they are also for instructing them in what they should do to please God, and live wholesome, fruitful, and joyful lives.

In applying these five aspects of Scriptures, the man of God is made "perfect, throughly furnished unto all good works." The word "perfect" does not mean sinless perfection; it means completed, or fully matured. Paul wrote in Philippians 3:12-15, *"Not as though I had already attained, either were already perfect: but I follow after . . . I count not myself to have apprehended* [perfection]: *but this one thing I do, forgetting those things which are behind, and reaching forth unto those things which are before, I* press toward the mark for the prize of the high calling of God in Christ Jesus. Let us therefore, as many as be perfect, be thus minded. . . ." To be made perfect through the study of the Scriptures is to forget our past mistakes and sins, and to fulfill the new mission in life that God has given us through Christ Jesus.

The phrase "throughly furnished unto all good works" means to thoroughly fit or equip a workman, for example a carpenter, with the right tools to do his job. If a building contractor hired a carpenter to help build a house, and the carpenter reported for work without a saw, a hammer, a square, or any tools at all, then he would not be any good to his employer. Likewise, without a thorough knowledge of the Scriptures, a Christian cannot do the job that Jesus Christ has called him to do.

Chapter Four

"I charge thee therefore before God, and the Lord Jesus Christ, who shall judge the quick and the dead at his appearing and his kingdom; Preach the word; be instant in season, out of season; reprove, rebuke, exhort with all longsuffering and doctrine. For the time will come when they will not endure sound doctrine; but after their own lusts shall they heap to themselves teachers, having itching ears; And they shall turn away their ears from the truth, and shall be turned unto fables" (2 Tim. 4:1-4).

In the fourth chapter, Paul places Timothy before the Judgment Seat of Christ. He writes, *"I charge thee therefore before God, and the Lord Jesus Christ, who shall judge the quick and the dead at his appearing and his kingdom."* The inference here is that if Timothy, in his high calling and responsibility to God, was not faithful and dedicated, he would have to give an account to Jesus Christ at the Judgment Seat.

In this charge to Timothy we find a parenthetical thought that we must first consider. It is Paul's reference to Jesus Christ judging both the quick and the dead at His appearing in His kingdom, meaning when He comes again. The *Bema*, or Seat of Judgment, is the judgment of Christians by Jesus Christ for their works, or deeds done in the flesh. Heaven or Hell is not a consideration. Christians who have done good works for the Lord after they are saved will receive a reward, or rewards. This judgment of believers will be soon after the rapture, and this is the judgment of the quick. Quick, as used in the context of judgment, means those who are alive in Jesus Christ. The dead means those who are spiritually dead — the unsaved dead. Although Paul mentions the judgment of both the quick and the dead in the same sentence, this does not mean that the judgment of both will come at the same time. The judgment of the quick, or saved, will be at the beginning of the Kingdom age reign of Jesus Christ. The judgment of the dead will come at the end of the Kingdom age. The separation of the judgment of the quick and the dead by one thousand years is clearly presented in Revelation 20:5-6, ". . . *the rest of the dead lived not again until the thousand years were finished. This* [meaning the resurrection mentioned in the previous verse] *is the first resurrection. Blessed and holy is he that hath part in the first resurrection: on such the second death hath no power. . . ."* The resurrection and judgment of the unsaved dead are also set forth in Revelation 20:12 as being at the end of the one thousand-year reign of Jesus Christ, *"And I saw the dead, small and great, stand before God. . . ."*

Only the lost dead will be judged at the Great White Throne Judgment, also known as the Last Judgment.

However, Paul cautions Timothy that in order to obtain a full reward, he must remain faithful in the following charges:

1. *Preach the Word* — the first duty of every minister is to preach the Word. Dr. Kenneth Wuest explains:

   "The word 'Word' here refers to the whole body of revealed truth, as will be seen by comparing this passage with 1 Thessalonians 1:6 and Galatians 6:6. The preacher must present, not book reviews, not politics, not economics, not current topics of the day, not a philosophy of life denying the Bible and based upon unproved theories of science, but the Word. The preacher as a herald cannot choose his message. He is given a message to proclaim by His Sovereign. If he will not proclaim that, let him step down from his exalted position."

2. *Be instant in season* — the charge here means to stand by, to be ready at all times when the opportunity presents itself to preach the Word of God.

3. *Be instant out of season* — the minister must also be ready to preach the Word at inopportune times. For example, a minister must be ready to preach in an air-conditioned auditorium, or under a tree in the country; in cold weather or hot weather; where there are five thousand in attendance, or only five in a home; whether he receives a large honorarium, or

a humble love offering. The meaning here is the minister must always be ready to preach, regardless of the circumstances.

4. *Reprove* — the minister must always use the Word of God to reprove. The meaning here is to bring the unsaved to a confession of their lost condition, or the Christian to repent and turn from committing sins. The minister is not only to deal with the sin questions in the lives of the unsaved, but also reprove the saints to forsake their sins.

5. *Rebuke* — rebuke is a stronger word than reprove. When a sinner continues to ignore the teachings and admonitions of the minister or other Christians, to forsake his ungodliness, then it becomes the duty of the pastor to condemn the sin in his life, possibly withdrawing fellowship until there is evidence of repentance.

6. *Exhort* — exhort means to plead with, encourage, or challenge the membership to greater efforts for the Lord Jesus Christ. This is the most wearisome part of the ministry of pastors — to try to stir up cold and indifferent Christians to witness to the lost.

7. *Watch in all things* — the meaning here is to watch over the church membership as a shepherd watches over his sheep. Always be on guard for wolves who try to snatch the sheep away, or for those who, like sheep, wander off and become lost in the world.

8. *Endure afflictions* — the constant reminder of Paul to Timothy may have been based, at least in part, on

past experience. Paul was in prison for the greater part of eight years, and Timothy was in prison with him for part of this time, probably about two years. It could be that prison life was extremely difficult for Timothy to bear, and for this reason Paul encourages him again and again to be mentally prepared to suffer afflictions for preaching the Word.

9. *Do the work of an evangelist* — always have as the primary reason for every message the leading of souls to faith in Jesus Christ. Also, be ready to go to evangelistic meetings. There were evangelists in those days (Acts 21:8; Eph. 4:11), and the minister of God, regardless of his calling, must always be ready to preach salvation to the unsaved.

10. *Make full proof of your ministry* — Jesus said that by their fruits they would be known. We read also in 2 Peter 1:10, *"Wherefore the rather, brethren, give diligence to make your calling and election sure. . . ."* All Christians are born again to work, as we read in Ephesians 2:10, *"For we are his workmanship, created in Christ Jesus unto good works, which God hath before ordained that we should walk in them."* Where there are no works, there is no proof of salvation. If a man says that he is called to be a pastor, and no pastoral works results, then we have reason to doubt his calling. A pastor or minister by scriptural definition will preach the Word, be ready to serve under any condition or situation, reprove, rebuke, exhort the

membership, watch over the flock, and be ready to suffer for Christ's sake.

These are the ten main considerations for a pastor set forth by the Apostle Paul, whom God called to preach to the Gentiles. Nothing is said about salary, an associate pastor, a new parsonage, a car allowance, insurance, or retirement. The church today has departed from the strict and sure guidelines for full-time Christian service. It is no wonder that the second part that Paul saw in the future is now coming to pass, "... *the time will come when they will not endure sound doctrine; but after their own lusts shall they heap to themselves teachers, having itching ears; And they shall turn away their ears from the truth, and shall be turned unto fables"* (2 Tim. 4:3-4).

In verses three and four of the fourth chapter, Paul looks down through the Church age by revelation from God, and sees the time when the majority of the churches will become carnal and seek teachers and preachers who will justify them in their own lusts. These apostate leaders will turn the truth of God, as set forth in the Bible, into fables or fiction.

Such is the condition of most churches today. Few congregations today hear strong doctrinal sermons and messages that will exhort, reprove, and rebuke the Christians to more dedicated service and godly living. Today, most want to hear messages that will tickle their ears rather than scorch their conscience. However, Paul said this time would come and we are seeing this prophecy being fulfilled today.

We continue in our study and read 2 Timothy 4:6-8:

> *"For I am now ready to be offered, and the time of my departure is at hand. I have fought a good fight, I have finished my course, I have kept the faith: Henceforth there is laid up for me a crown of righteousness, which the Lord, the righteous judge, shall give me at that day: and not to me only, but unto all them also that love his appearing."*

In verse six, Paul wrote to Timothy, "I am now ready to be offered." The word offered used here in the Greek language means a libation, or a drink offering. This means that he was reconciled to the fact that he was to be beheaded — his blood poured out. Nero had either already judged Paul, or at least the apostle had no hope for mercy from Caesar. Being a Roman citizen, Paul had a right by law to make a final appeal to the emperor, but in his case it was to no avail. However, being a Roman citizen he would not suffer the cruel and inhuman death of crucifixion or be thrown into the arena with wild beasts. His death would be by beheading, and according to tradition, this is the way he died. Dr. Kenneth Wuest says of the departure:

> *"The simple meaning of the word is to*

> *unloose, undo again, break up. It was a common expression for death, and it was used in military circles of the taking down of a tent and the departure of an army, and in nautical language, of the hoisting of an anchor and the sailing of a ship."*

In other words, it was time for Paul to take down his tent and leave for another place. The two expressions, "I have fought a good fight, I have finished my course," indicate athletic terminology. Like a wrestler, he had fought as hard as he could and with all his ability, and he had now finished his course, or completed his race. Unless he had finished his course, or did everything that God had willed that he do, Nero could not have taken his life. In saying that he had "kept the faith" he meant that he had safe-guarded the body of truth, the gospel, against all those who would try to destroy it or pervert it with false doctrine. He had protected it with his very life.

Dake's Annotated Reference Bible has this interesting note on the final statement of Paul concerning his impending death:

1. *Ready to be offered or poured out as a libation to God and a sacrifice offering for souls.*
2. *My departure is at hand — the sentence of death had already been passed.*
3. *I have fought a good fight: an honorable fight — wrestled a good wrestling and am champion.*

4. I have finished my course — run the race and have
   outstripped all my competitors and gained a prize.
5. I have kept the faith — followed every rule of the
   game and have won the prize lawfully.

Verse eight mentions the crown for fighting a good fight and for finishing the course. I have been at Corinth where the original Grecian olympic games were held. In the ruins of the old coliseum, the arena where the wrestlers, javelin and discus throwers competed and the track where the runners ran is still much in evidence. At one side of the arena, the old Bema seat is clearly marked, and here a judge of the contestants sat and awarded the winners a crown of ivy or oak leaves. Paul avers that inasmuch as he has competed and emerged a winner, there will be a righteous or just Judge to appraise his efforts, and he was confident that he too would win a crown — a crown of righteousness. The "crown of righteousness" is one of the rewards that will be given by our righteous Judge, the Lord Jesus Christ, at the Judgment Seat where Christians will be judged for their works. According to Paul, the crown of righteousness will be given to those who love the appearing of Jesus. The word for appearing in the Greek was used to describe the visible appearing, or manifestation, of the Grecian gods and goddesses. It looks forward, literally, to the appearing of Jesus Christ in His glory, His second coming with the angels of Heaven. There are many Christians today who will not receive this reward because they are willingly ignorant of His return and will not even discuss it.

> *"Do thy diligence to come shortly unto me:*
> *For Demas hath forsaken me, having loved*
> *the present world, and is departed unto*
> *Thessalonica; Crescens to Galatia, Titus*
> *unto Dalmatia"* (2 Tim. 4:9-10).

Paul urged Timothy to come to him as quickly as he could, because he knew his time was short. He longed to see Timothy, whom he dearly loved, one more time. It was very human and natural for Paul to have desired Timothy's companionship, and the comfort he could give him in his last days.

Demas had let Paul down and abandoned him when he needed him most. Demas was one of the brethren at Thessalonica who went with Paul and he is mentioned in Philemon 1:24 as being with the apostle at Rome when he was first imprisoned. He is again mentioned in Colossians 2:14 as being with Paul and Luke. To his credit, Demas must have stayed with Paul until after the death penalty was given by Nero. It was then that he decided to return to Thessalonica to resume his family life and occupation. However, the wording here in the Greek text brings out that he left Paul at a critical time and it was a cruel blow to be deserted in his time of greatest need.

Although Paul makes no special negative statements against Crescens and Titus, it is evident that they acted on their own initiative, possibly feeling they were needed elsewhere.

We continue and read 2 Timothy 4:11-12:

"Only Luke is with me. Take Mark, and bring him with thee: for he is profitable to me for the ministry. And Tychicus have I sent to Ephesus."

What a testimony to the love and grace of God was Luke, the beloved physician. He was with Paul throughout his ordeal. Here was a Greek physician who left his practice to become the personal doctor of an itinerant preacher of Jewish birth. Whenever Paul was stoned or beaten, Luke was there to care for his wounds. His medical instinct kept him by Paul's side to render what medical aid he could, right to the very end. What a comfort and friend he must have been to the apostle.

Timothy was also to bring Mark with him to see Paul before he died. Mark had deserted Paul and Barnabas in Cyprus, and afterward he was reluctant to take the young disciple with him. However, Mark had matured with age and later proved to be a profitable servant. From this reference to Mark, we know that Paul must have later considered him to be a valuable minister of the Lord Jesus.

Tychicus was from Asia and is mentioned several times in Paul's epistles. We read in Ephesians 6:21 that Paul considered Tychicus "a beloved brother and faithful minister in the Lord" and in the same verse he said that he had sent him to Ephesus to make known unto the church there the status of the apostle's affairs and to strengthen their faith in Jesus Christ. Timothy was also at Ephesus, so we assume that he was already aware that Paul had dispatched Tychicus there for a purpose. He evidently wanted to clear Tychicus from any suspicions that he had also deserted Paul.

We next read 2 Timothy 4:13:

"The cloke that I left at Troas with Carpus, when thou comest, bring with thee, and the books, but especially the parchments."

The cloak that Paul asked Timothy to bring with him was a type that was made of goat's hair. It was called a *kepenickler* and it was worn by shepherds to keep out the wind and the rain. In Rome, winter was approaching, and Paul needed it in the cold and damp prison to help keep him warm.

The books that Paul requested to be brought were actually papyrus rolls. These rolls of stiff, cardboard-like paper were made from reeds that grew along the Nile. In Egypt today, these papyrus rolls are still made as a novelty item to be sold to tourists. But in Paul's day, papyrus paper was a valuable commercial item for Egypt, and was sold throughout the Mediterranean area and the Middle East. The parchments that Paul wanted were made from the skins of sheep, goats, or antelopes. Parchments were much more durable then papyrus. The Scriptures that were written on parchments lasted, while those written on papyrus were lost. So Paul especially wanted the parchments. It was evident that he intended to write more epistles, but it is not known if he did or not. Also, there is no evidence that Timothy returned to Rome, or if he did, that he reached Paul before his death.

> *"Alexander the coppersmith did me much evil: the Lord reward him according to his works: Of whom be thou ware also; for he hath greatly withstood our words"* (2 Tim. 4:14-15).

Little is known about Alexander. He must have been a metal worker at Ephesus and probably was the same Alexander of Ephesus mentioned in Acts 19:33-34. Although he was a Jew, he made idols of Diana for profit. It would seem that Paul witnessed to him, but Alexander did not repent and helped to add to Paul's persecution at the hands of the idol worshippers. Paul did not attempt to repay Alexander, but left his punishment to the Lord. Paul wrote in Romans 12:19, *"Dearly beloved, avenge not yourselves, but rather give place unto wrath: for it is written, Vengeance is mine; I will repay, saith the Lord."*

We continue by reading 2 Timothy 4:16-18:

> *"At my first answer no man stood with me, but all men forsook me: I pray God that it*

may not be laid to their charge. Notwith-standing the Lord stood with me, and strengthened me; that by me the preaching might be fully known, and that all the Gentiles might hear: and I was delivered out of the mouth of the lion. And the Lord shall deliver me from every evil work, and will preserve me unto his heavenly kingdom: to whom be glory for ever and ever. Amen."

In verse sixteen, Paul speaks of his trial before Nero. When a citizen accused of a crime stood before Caesar, it was Roman law that he must have someone speak up for him, or else he was sentenced without a hearing. When Paul appeared before Nero, no one, not even his closest friends and associates, had the courage to stand with him. All forsook him. The *Greek New Testament* by Wuest reads:

"During my self defense at the preliminary trial, not even one person appeared in court, taking his stand at my side as a friend of mine, but all let me down."

Nevertheless, Paul was not alone. He had a friend in court, the Lord Jesus Christ. Jesus promised His disciples, *". . . lo, I am with you alway, even unto the end of the world"* (Matt. 28:20). And so in spite of the fact that Paul had to face Nero alone, his wording here illustrates that he did have his say in court. We can be sure just as Paul preached the gospel to Festus, to Felix, and to Herod, he also told Nero how to be saved. Nero cannot stand in the last judgment and say he was never told that Jesus Christ died for his sins. The phrase "delivered out of the mouth of the lion" means to escape the devil's trap. Peter described the devil as a roaring lion, and in the messianic psalms, the Lord Jesus is depicted as praying for deliverance from the lion as He hung on the cross.

Paul had encountered every evil persecution that could be devised by wicked men, yet the apostle said they all failed in their vain iniquity, because nothing on earth could prevent his entrance into the heavenly kingdom of Jesus Christ. This is the Christian's consolation. Paul's assurance of eternal salvation is clearly established in all of his epistles. We read in Hebrews 7:25, "*. . . he is able also to save them to the uttermost that come unto God by him. . . .*"

We complete our study by reading 2 Timothy 4:19-22:

> "*Salute Prisca and Aquila, and the household of Onesiphorus. Erastus abode at Corinth: but Trophimus have I left at Miletum sick. Do thy diligence to come before winter. Eubulus greeteth thee, and Pudens, and Linus, and Claudia, and all the brethren. The Lord Jesus Christ be with thy spirit. Grace be with you. Amen.*"

Priscilla and Aquila and their ministry are noted

in several places in Acts, Romans, and 1 Corinthians. We have already commented on the household of Onesiphorus in our study of the first chapter of 2 Timothy. Erastus was the treasurer of Corinth. Trophimus accompanied Paul on his third missionary journey, and he later was beheaded by Nero also. Eubulus was a Christian at Rome and a friend of Paul. Some believe that he was the first evangelist to go to England. Pudens was a loyal Roman Christian. There is evidence that Pudens and Claudia were of the royal family of Rome, and Linus their son later become bishop of Rome.

Paul preached the gospel to the Gentile world in response to his calling, but it is also noteworthy that with his last written words he noted specific individuals. Because he loved people, he could not have done otherwise. Likewise, God, who is the Creator and Ruler of the universe, is concerned with people. God is concerned about the individual. He is concerned about you. We read in John 3:16, *"For God so loved the world, that he gave his only begotten Son, that whosoever believeth in him should not perish, but have everlasting life."*